FRANZ ROSENTHAL

A GRAMMAR OF BIBLICAL ARAMAIC

PORTA LINGUARUM ORIENTALIUM

HERAUSGEGEBEN VON BERTOLD SPULER UND HANS WEHR

NEUE SERIE

V

FRANZ ROSENTHAL

A GRAMMAR
OF BIBLICAL ARAMAIC

FOURTH PRINTING

1974

OTTO HARRASSOWITZ · WIESBADEN

A GRAMMAR
OF BIBLICAL ARAMAIC

BY

FRANZ ROSENTHAL

FOURTH **PRINTING**

1974

OTTO HARRASSOWITZ · WIESBADEN

ISBN 3 447 00688 9

Table of Contents

Preface

The purpose of this grammar is twofold. It is, on the one hand, to provide the beginner with the elements of the language, and, on the other, to prepare him—surreptitiously as it were—for possible research in the problems of Aramaeology. These two aims may seem mutually contradictory, and it must be admitted that they are to a degree. However, the attempt is always worth making, and Biblical Aramaic, representing the comparative simplicity of the old consonant writing with the complexities of a much later stage of the spoken language superimposed upon it, is a strenuous training ground.

Biblical Aramaic grammars are customarily written in the assumption that the reader will have previously acquired a good knowledge of Biblical Hebrew. This assumption may be correct, but it seems a poor justification for not giving Biblical Aramaic its due as a language in its own right. Therefore, no knowledge of Hebrew is presupposed here. Brevity has made it necessary to deal lightly with many of the Masoretic refinements, and no lengthy discussions of Semitic peculiarities, let alone comparative excursuses, were possible. But the presentation, it is hoped, will be clear for the student with or without much grounding in other Semitic languages.

Knowledge of the syntax is important in any language, and in Aramaic where the syntax in particular reflects the history of the language most faithfully, it is of crucial significance. I have taken cognizance of this fact by *not* writing a special discussion of Biblical Aramaic syntax, since I know that few beginning students of a language ever take the trouble of reading the portion of the grammar dealing with syntax. Instead, the most important syntactic notions have been added to appropriate passages of the grammatical treatment. This often involves anticipating linguistic points not yet discussed, but I believe that the reader will not find this unduly disturbing.

The basis of this grammar is the text as published in the "Kittel Bible," that is, the third edition of the *Biblia Hebraica*

(Stuttgart, 1937), originally organized by R. Kittel. The text of
Ezra was prepared by H. H. Schaeder, and that of Daniel by
W. Baumgartner. Subsequent editions—I have before me one la-
beled the ninth being a reproduction of the seventh (Stuttgart, 1954)—contain no changes in the Aramaic portions. As
this is the most authoritative text presently available, it is imperative here to follow it to the letter. Even details of orthography and vocalization are nearly always accepted as they appear
in the *Biblia Hebraica*. However, it should be realized that
manuscript variations as far as orthography and vocalization
are concerned are numerous and important, and the text of
the *Biblia Hebraica* does not constitute the last word with
regard to them. Moreover, while the work of the Masoretes is
most remarkable for its linguistic accuracy and reliability, most
of the progress in our understanding of the contents and the
languages of the Bible depends on our increasing ability of going
beyond it.

Very little, if anything, that is new will be found in this grammar.
There exist some good grammars by outstanding scholars and one
recent, excellent dictionary. However, there should be room for
one more attempt to help students to acquire a basic preparation
in a language that holds the key to a good deal of the world's
intellectual history, and I am extremely grateful to the publisher
and the editors of the *Porta* that they have given me the opportunity
to make this attempt. I also had the good fortune of being able to
draw upon the knowledge of several outstanding authorities. First
among them was H. L. Ginsberg with whom I was privileged to
discuss my manuscript and who made many substantial contribu-
tions. A further reading of the manuscript by F. M. Cross proved
most helpful and yielded valuable suggestions. A reading of the
proofs by M. Pope contributed important corrections and improve-
ments. The section on Akkadian loan words (par. 188) has greatly
benefitted from the advice of A. Goetze, and the section on
Persian loan words (par. 189f.) and the Persian etymologies in the
glossary were revised by W. B. Henning who thus did for this
grammar what F. C. Andreas did many years ago for its predecessor
in the *Porta*.

*   *
*

Few abbreviations have been used. They are either self-evident
or have been explained in the proper places. An asterisk is used to
indicate forms or form elements not attested in Biblical Aramaic;
two asterisks occasionally indicate that the form-elements so
marked are not known from other Official Aramaic texts either,
but they have not been used consistently. No asterisks have been
used in connection with the paradigms. In transliterations, primary
and secondary word stress is indicated by ´ and `, respectively
(par. 28). An arbitrary sign ≤ has been chosen to indicate penult
stress in Aramaic writing (par. 26).

*   *
*

In the second printing, only a few minor changes have been
made. For some corrections I am indebted to the reviews of
H. L. Ginsberg (in *Journal of Biblical Literature*, LXXX [1961],
386 f.) and H. Michaud (in *Syria*, XXXVIII [1961], 327 ff.);
others were brought to my attention by M. Pope and Rabbi
T. Gluck.

*   *
*

For the third printing, the bibliography on pp. 72—75 has been
brought up to date.

*   *
*

Changes made in the bibliography for the fourth printing have
been more numerous, without, however, my being able to do
justice to the intensive and productive interest in Aramaic studies
during recent years.

I. The Texts and the Language

1. Aramaic passages occur in the Old Testament in four places:

Ezra 4:8—6:18 and 7:12—26 (documents from the Achaemenid period concerning the restoration of the temple in Jerusalem).

Daniel 2:4—7:28 (five Oriental historical tales involving Jews and an apocalyptic vision).

Jer. 10:11 (a stray Aramaic sentence in a Hebrew context denouncing idolatry).

Gen. 31:47 (two words translating a Hebrew toponym into Aramaic said to be the language of Laban).

Certain Hebrew texts of the Bible have been recognized as translations from an Aramaic original.

2. The native name of the language was Aramaic. This is indicated by the (Hebrew) gloss $^{\jmath a}r\bar{a}m\bar{\imath}\underline{t}$ E 4:7, D 2:4, introducing Aramaic passages in about the same manner in which Aramaic papyri from Egypt use, for instance, $m\d{s}ryt$ to indicate use of an Egyptian term.

3. The Aramaic texts of the Bible come from periods separated, approximately, by as much as three centuries. They represent different types of literature. They were written by men belonging to different strata of society. And, in all likelihood, they originated in different localities. Yet, the language they use appears to all intents and purposes uniform, with only minor divergences. This strange fact is explained by the history of Aramaic.

The earliest Aramaic inscriptions discovered so far come from the ninth century B. C. At the beginning of our era, Aramaic, in various dialectal forms, was the dominant spoken language of Syria and Mesopotamia. It developed a number of literary dialects, known as Palestinian Jewish Aramaic, Samaritan, and Syro-Palestinian Christian Aramaic along the Eastern border of the Mediterranean, and Syriac, Babylonian Talmudic Aramaic, and Mandaic in Mesopotamia. To this day, there are small groups that speak Aramaic dialects, such as the inhabitants of some villages in the Anti-Lebanon, Christians and Jews living in or originating from

Azerbaijan and Kurdistan, to which may be added remnants of the gnostic sect of the Mandaeans, familiar with the tradition of their dialect.

During the second millennium B. C., various Aramaic dialects are likely to have been spoken at the borders and within Mesopotamia and the Fertile Crescent. But it was the dialect used by Aramaeans settled within the confines of Assyria that from the eighth century on supplanted all other Aramaic dialects. According to 2 Kings 18:26, Aramaic was, at the end of that century, an international language understood by high Assyrian and Jewish officials but not by the common people of Jerusalem. When the Achaemenids conquered Mesopotamia in the second half of the sixth century and established their vast empire, they continued the use of Aramaic as the medium for written communication in their far-flung administration. By that time, Aramaic was the dominant spoken language in Mesopotamia. It was making steady headway as a spoken language in the lands of the Fertile Crescent, including Palestine.

The use of this "Official Aramaic" of the Achaemenid Empire outlasted the latter's existence by some centuries. Official Aramaic, when written by people whose native language was not Aramaic, showed considerable divergences in a number of aspects, especially in the syntax and the vocabulary. When it was used by native speakers of Aramaic, local dialectal differences made themselves felt. At first, these were inconspicuous, but they grew more and more pronounced with the political and religious fragmentation of the Aramaic speaking area, and eventually made their appearance as distinct dialects.

The Aramaic of the Bible as written has preserved the Official Aramaic character. This is what makes it nearly uniform in linguistic appearance. It also makes it largely identical with the language used in other Official Aramaic texts. Most numerous among these are the Aramaic documents of the Achaemenid period discovered in Egypt which are invaluable for the understanding of Biblical Aramaic (henceforth abbreviated BA).

II. The Writing

4. The letters of the BA alphabet are the same as are used in Hebrew. The so-called Hebrew or square script is, in fact, a Jewish specialization of the older Official Aramaic script adopted by the

Egypt 5th cent. B.C.	Dead Sea Scrolls (Qumrān) 1st cent. B.C. to 1st cent. A.D.	Trans-litera-tion	Name	Approximate Pronunciation
א	א	ʾ	ʾālep̄	glottal stop
ב	ב	b, b̲	bēṯ	b, spirant b (bilabial v)
ג	ג	g, ḡ	gimel	g, spirant g
ד	ד	d, ḏ	dāleṯ	d, spirant d (like *th* in *there*)
ה	ה	h	hē	h
ו	ו	w	wāw	w
ז	ז	z	zayin	z
ח	ח	ḥ	ḥēṯ	pharyngal fricative h
ט	ט	ṭ	ṭēṯ	"emphatic" (i.e., velarized) t
י	י	y	yōḏ	y
כ (ך)	ך	k, k̲	kap̄	k, spirant k
ל	ל	l	lāmeḏ	l
מ (ם)	מ ם	m	mēm	m
נ (ן)	ן נ	n	nūn	n
ס	ס	s	sāmek̲	s
ע	ע	ʿ	ʿayin	voiced laryngal (similar to the sound of incipient vomiting)
פ (ף)	ף פ	p, p̄	pē	p, spirant p (bilabial f)
צ (ץ)	ץ צ	ṣ	ṣāḏē	"emphatic" s
ק	ק	q	qōp̄	"emphatic" k
ר	ר	r	rēš	r
שׂ	שׂ	ś	śīn	palatalized (?) s
שׁ	שׁ	š	šīn	sh
ת	ת	t, ṯ	tāw	t, spirant t (like *th* in *think*)

2 Rosenthal, Grammar

Jews in the course of their acceptance of Official Aramaic and the increasing use of Aramaic as a spoken language among them.

The writing runs from right to left.

The forms of the letters in brackets are those occurring at the end of a word.

The names of the letters are those commonly used in Hebrew grammar.

5. אהוי may be used as vowel letters (par. 10). א and ה are used for final $\bar{a}$ or $\bar{e}$, ו for $\bar{u}$ or $\bar{o}$, and י for $\bar{\imath}$ and $\bar{e}$. Final $\bar{e}$, which occurs very rarely, is indicated by ה.

א appears as vowel letter in connection with final $\bar{o}$ in לְגוֹא "into" and the proper name עַדּוֹא. This use is frequent in later Jewish Aramaic documents and appears to have resulted from the spelling of (Hebrew) לֹא (לוֹא) "not." Note that the Dead Sea (Qumrān) fragment of D 3:24 has לגו, although the spelling וא- for final $\bar{o}$ is common in the Dead Sea documents. Cf., further, par. 13.

6. The final forms כנפצ are the earlier forms of these letters. The forms used within words represent a later development. The closed form of final ם, on the other hand, is derived from the older open מ. The consistent distinction between final and non-final letters appears to be not earlier than the third century B. C.

In the Egyptian documents and the Dead Sea material, words are separated from each other by a clearly noticeable blank space. Exceptions are rare. The same situation no doubt prevailed when the BA texts were committed to writing.

7. Consonant doubling (par. 20) is indicated by a dot placed in the geminated letter.

A dot is also used to indicate non-spirantized pronunciation of בגדכפת (par. 15).

It occurs further in connection with final ה in order to indicate that it is not used as a vowel letter but is to be pronounced as a consonant.

8. Ancient Aramaic developed an incomplete system of indicating vowels by using certain consonants (par. 5). This started with final long vowels but was soon extended to internal long vowels (except $\bar{a}$). The Biblical text shows a more systematic but still far from consistent application of this kind of vocalization (par. 10, 13).

The use of special vowel signs for the Biblical text is of a much later date. It is in general not earlier than the seventh century A.D. The men who provided the Biblical texts with vowels signs are known as Masoretes ("transmitters"). Their efforts began with occasional indications of some vowels but developed into systems meant to be a complete (and rather complicated) phonetic notation.

There are three vowel systems known, the Palestinian, the Babylonian, and the Tiberian. The one in use in our Bible texts is the Tiberian. There are many small differences in vocalization within the various manuscripts and systems of vocalization.

The systems of vocalization were invented primarily for the Hebrew text. Influence of Hebrew phonetic peculiarities upon the vocalization of BA may be assumed on occasion. However, since the phonetic habits of the Masoretes were formed by Aramaic speech, their systems of vocalization may be assumed rather to represent Aramaic speech habits.

The Tiberian system favors the Palestinian pronunciation of Aramaic. The Babylonian system leans toward that of Mesopotamia; notwithstanding its importance, little attention has perforce been paid to it in this grammar. BA texts with Palestinian vocalization are not available.

In the Tiberian system, the vowel sign is placed underneath the letter that is followed by the vowel in question. An exception is the vowel $\bar{o}$ which is placed on top and to the left of the letter.

Final vowelless החע, after a long vowel other than $\bar{a}$, are furnished with an a vowel placed a little to the right, indicating a preceding ultra-short ^{a} that is heard when the consonants in question are pronounced correctly (-$^a\d{h}$, -$^a{}^c$; there is no example for -h).

In the Babylonian (and Palestinian) systems, the vowel signs are placed on top of the consonants.

9. The vowel signs do not indicate vowel quantity (length or brevity) but vowel quality. For a proper understanding of the attempt made in the following paragraph to distinguish between long and short vowels, it will be well to keep in mind that the Semitic languages know extremely stable long vowels used to indicate certain basic noun and verb formations. All the other vowels are exceedingly unstable and run the gamut from ultra-shortness to what at times may strike the listener as almost a long

vowel. The Masoretes aspired to catching and noting down the
finest vowel shades such as were due to the influence of surrounding
consonants, word and sentence stress, etc. This is a very difficult
task that can be successfully accomplished only for a living language
under carefully controlled conditions. How far the subtle Masoretic
distinctions are applicable to the pre-Masoretic period of BA
remains doubtful.

10. These are the Tiberian vowel signs:

ְ indicates vowellessness. Final vowelless consonants have no such
sign, with the exception of ךְ and תְּ.

Since vowellessness in BA is very frequently the result of the
disappearance of short vowels, it may not always have been
complete but a murmured vowel may have remained, especially
where otherwise there would have appeared consonant clusters
that were hard to pronounce. In such cases, we cannot decide
whether there was vowellessness or a murmured vowel. The sign
ᵊ has been used for transliterating them.

The sign ְ may be combined with one of the following three
vowel signs in order to indicate ultra-short vowels: ֲ ^{a}; ֳ ^{o}; ֱ ^{e}.
These are used in connection with אהחע instead of simple ְ,
whenever it is in the place of an original vowel. But they may
also occur in positions where there was no vowel originally
(לֶהֱוֵא "he will be," לְהַחֲוָיָה "to inform," אָחֳרָן "another," מַעֲבָדׄוהִי
"His works").

They may also be used following or preceding ק and ג, or
preceding לנר : קְדָם "before," לָקֳבֵל "corresponding to," קְרִי
"it was read" E 4:18, 23, מַדְקָה, מַדֱקָה "crushing" D 7:7, 19,
גְלִי, גֱלִי "it was revealed" D 2:19, 30, סְגַר "he locked" D 6:23,
מְמַלְלָה "speaking" D 7:11, בֱנַיְתֵה "I built it" D 4:27, צִפֲרֵי
"birds" D 4:9.

ַ _a_ (short).

ָ _ā_. Original long _ā_ must have been pronounced by the Masoretes
like long open _o_, since its short form is _o_ (short) in the following
cases:

(1) in closed unstressed syllables: כָּרְסָא "chair," דָּכְרָנַיָּא
(_dokrānayyā_) "memoranda," פָּלְחָן (_polḥān_) "cult," כָּל קֳבֵל
(_kol qᵒbel_) "corresponding to."

(2) when followed by $-$, or by $-$ in a closed unstressed syllable: לְקֳבֵל (loqᵒḇēl), הָחָרְבַת (hoḥorḇat) "was destroyed."

(3) when it represents $-$ under secondary stress in the preposition קֳדָם "before": קֳדָמַי (qŏḏāmáy) "before me," but קֳדָמֵיהֹן (qᵒḏămēhŏn) "before them."

(4) possibly in תְּקָף "strength" D 4:27.

$-$ e (open, short). In אֵלֶּה "these," it may possibly represent a long vowel. For עֲלֵינָא, cf. par. 49, and for נִדְנֶה, cf. par. 190.

e is very close to a, cf., for instance, יְדְהֹם "their hand" E 5:8, for *יֶדְהֹם, or אֲחֵיךְ "your brothers (colleagues)," for אֲחִיךְ (par. 62). The Babylonian system has no sign for it but uses a. However, e also occurs as a variant of ẹ/i (יֶפֵּל, but יִפֵּל לָךְ yippelláḵ, par. 118).

$-$ ẹ, ē̦ (closed). Most frequently, $-$ represents short ẹ, as in בְּעֵל "master," הוֹתֵב "he settled," etc., also in cases where it alternates with i (יִתְעֲבֵד, יִתְעֲבֵד "will be made").

Secondary lengthening may have been operative in some of these cases. Lengthening may also be assumed where $-$ appears in unstressed open syllables (par. 23): עֵטָה "counsel," לְחֵנָתֵה "his maids," גֵּוָה "arrogance," יְקֵדַת "burning." This, however, is not certain since $-$ in בְּטֵלַת (bᵉṭẹlát) "was idle" E 4:24, is certainly short.

$-$ represents a long vowel at the ends of words when it is followed by one of the vowel letters אהי; or, within words, when it is followed by the vowel letter י; or where it represents the result of the sound change ẹ/i' > ē̦ (לְמֵאמַר "to say," לְמֵזֵא "to heat," בֵּאדַיִן "then," etc.).

$-$ i, ī. Long ī is as a rule followed by the vowel letter י. There are exceptions such as מְדִנָן "provinces" E 4:15, כְּפִתוּ "they were fettered" D 3:21, שַׁלִּטִן "mighty" (pl. masc.) D 4:23, זִוִי "my splendor, splendid looks" D 4:33. The more remarkable use of י where short i is required appears in מַשְׁפִּיל "bringing down" D 5:19, הַלְבִּישׁוּ "they dressed" D 5:29, קְרִיבוּ "they drew near" D 6:13, שֵׁיזִיב "he saved" D 6:28.

$-$ ǫ, ō̦ (closed), as a long vowel usually combined with the vowel letter ו (ŏ), but occasionally occurring without it, in particular after -w (-wō̦). It may appear in stressed syllables which when they are not stressed would exhibit short *o* or *u*: קְשֹׁט "truth," כֹּל "all," גֹב (גּוֹב D 6:13) "den." In these cases, a short but closed *ọ*, rather than a long vowel, may be intended. Short *ọ* in כֹּלָּא (*kọllā*) "totality," גֹּדּוּ (*gọddu*) "cut down!" (pl. masc.) D 4:11, אָרְחָתֵהּ "His ways."

٫ *u, ū*, as a long vowel usually expressed by the sign ו, but cf. לִבְשֵׁיהוֹן "their garments" D 3:21, לְהוֹדָעֻתַנִי "to let me know" D 2:26, etc. In תְּהוֹדְעֻנַּנִי "you let me know" D 2:5 and similar forms, *ū* may have been shortened in pronunciation but retained as a historical spelling; ו appears in these cases in the Aramaic documents from Egypt, whereas BA spelling vacillates between ו und ٫ (par. 175).

11. The signs of the Babylonian system are: ﹷ for vowellessness; ﹷ *a, e*; ﹷ *ā*; ﹷ *ẹ, ẹ̄*; ﹷ *i, ī*; ﹷ *ọ, ọ̄*; ﹷ *u, ū*.

12. *Kᵉt̲ib̲—Qᵉrẹ̄*: In a number of cases, according to the Masoretes, words "written" (*kᵉt̲ib̲*) in one way are to be "read" (*qᵉrẹ̄*) in another. Some of these are of considerable grammatical importance, as, for instance, אַנְתָּה (*ántā*, read *ant*) "you" (sg. masc.), דָּאְרִין (*dāᵉrin*, read *dāyᵉrin*) "dwelling" (part. pl. masc.), נְפַלוּ (*nᵉp̲álū*, read *nᵉp̲álā*) "they (fem.) fell" (where the *kᵉt̲ib̲* may, in fact, be a corruption of *נפלי*), etc.

The often expressed *a priori* assumption that the consonant text (*kᵉt̲ib̲*) represents the more original form of the text is, as far as BA is concerned, a dangerous oversimplification.

III. Remarks on Phonology

13. In addition to its use as a vowel letter at the ends of words (par. 5), א also occurs as a silent letter:

(1) in words where it became silent and was retained as a historical spelling: רֵאשׁ (< *riᵉš-*) "head," מָאנַיָּא (< *maᵉnayyā*) "vessels," מֹאזְנַיָה (= מֹאזְנַיָה, < *mawzan-*, spelled with א as in Hebrew) "scales" D 5:27, בָּאתַר (< *baᵉt̲ar*) "after" but בִּתְרָךְ D 2:39, מָאתַיִן (< *maᵉt-* < *miᵉat-*) "two hundred," דָּנִיֵּאל „Daniel," הוּא (*hū* < *huᵉa*) "he," הִיא (*hī* < *hiᵉa*) "she." The origin of the א in צַוְּארֵהּ (*ṣawwᵉrẹh*) "his neck" D 5:7 (as in Hebrew spelling) is not clear.

(2) in particular grammatical forms where it became silent: יֵאמַר (< *yiᵃmar*) "he says," לְמֵאמַר (< *miᵃmar*) "to say," but phonetic spellings are also found (מֵמַר, לְמֵתָא "to come," לְמֵזֵא "to heat"); לַאלָהָיִךְ (< *le*ᵃ-) "to your gods," בֵּאדָיִן (< *be*ᵃ-) "then."

(3) in final vowelless position, or after a zero or murmured vowel: שַׂגִּיא (*śaggi*), but שַׂגִּיאָן (*śaggiᵃān*) "much, many," בְּאִשְׁתָּא (*biśtā*) "evil" E 4:12, but בְּאֵשׁ (*baᵃēš*) "was bad" D 6:15, מָרִאי (*mārī*) "my lord," but שָׂנְאָיִךְ (*śānᵃᵃāk*) "your enemies" D 4:16.

(4) in the distorted pronunciation of foreign proper names: בֵּלְטְשַׁאצַּר (< *Balāṭ-šarri-uṣur?*), בֵּלְשַׁאצַּר, בֵּלְאשַׁצַּר (< *Bēl-šar-uṣur*).

14. א results occasionally from -*āy*-, as in כַּשְׂדָּיאָ (*Kaśdāᵃā* < *Kaśdāyā*) "Chaldaean," תְּלִיתָיא (*tᵉlitaᵃā* < *tᵉlitāyā*) "third" (fem.), קָאֵם (*qāᵃēm* < *qāyem*) "standing." Inversely, we find חֲטָיִךְ (*ḥᵃṭāyāk*) "your sins" D 4:24 for *חֲטָאִךְ (*ḥᵃṭāᵃāk*).

15. Spirantization of בגדכפת ("*bᵉḡaḏkᵉpaṯ*") is an Aramaic development which, in all likelihood, was under way in the sixth century B. C. It takes place after vowels and after zero or murmured vowels resulting from the disappearance of an original vowel. This includes forms such as מַלְכִין (< *malakin*) "kings," כִּדְבָה (< *kadabā*) "untrue" (fem.).

The ת of the fem. ending shows *t* rather than *ṯ* in בְּאִישְׁתָּא (*biśtā*) "evil" E 4:12, מְדִינְתָּא (*mᵉḏintā*) "province" E 5:8, 6:2, עֲבִידְתָּא (*ᶜᵃḇiḏtā*) "work" E 5:8, D 2:49, מָרָדְתָּא "rebellious" E 4:12, but בִּירְתָא "fortress" E 6:2. Spirantization is always found after *ē̦*: חֵיוְתָא "animal," שְׁאֵלְתָּא "question," אֵימְתַנִי "frightful." Note the spirantization of ג in the Persian loan word פִּתְגָם "message, word."

Spirantization also takes place after the diphthong -*ay*-: בַּיְתָא "house," הַיְתִי "he brought."

16. Within the sentence, בגדכפת (at the beginning of a word following a word ending in a vowel) are spirantized when the words in question are thought to be closely connected. In practice, such close connection is indicated by a short line connecting the letters at the top (for instance, דִּי־דְהַב), or by the use of a connecting "accent." The "accents," which are either "dividing" or "connecting," are special signs placed on top or underneath each word, usually but not always on the syllable receiving primary stress. Connecting accents requiring spirantization that occur in BA are:

ַ (but *not* | ַ), ָ (placed *after* the vowel sign), ְ, ֢ (but *not* ֢ placed upon the lāst consonant of the word), ֚ (placed upon the last consonant of the word), and ֚.

Occasional exceptions are admitted: בְּבָבֶל ַ "in Babylon" E 5:17, כְּחָכְמַת ָ (unstresssed) "like the wisdom of" D 5:11, in each case because of the sequence of three identical or similar consonants; דְּתָבְרַיָּא ַ "law officials" D 3:2, דְּתָבְרַיָּא ֚ D 3:3; פְּסַנְתֵּרִין ַ "psaltery" D 3:5, but פְּסַנְתֵּרִין ַ D 3:10 (this being a case much discussed by the Masoretes who appear to have been undecided how to fit the Greek letter into Aramaic speech habits).

As a rule, it is easy to see why in a given case close connection requiring spirantization is assumed, but no fixed rules can be given. The negation always requires spirantization for the following word. Demonstrative pronouns beginning with ד also show spirantization in connection with nouns to which they belong, an exception being, however, רָזָה דְנָה "this secret" D 2:18.

17. BA ח corresponds to two different phonemes of the original Semitic stock of consonants (*ḥ* and *ḫ* [*kh*]).

BA דטת each correspond to two, ע to three different phonemes of the original Semitic stock of consonants. ד corresponds to *d* and *ḏ*, ת to *t* and *ṯ*, ט to *ṭ* and *ṯ* (*ḏ*, *ẓ*), and ע to *ʿ*, *ḏ*, and *ġ*:

Semitic	Ugaritic	Hebrew	Aramaic	Arabic
d	d	ד	ד	د
ḏ	d	ז	ד	ذ
z	z	ז	ז	ز
t	t	ת	ת	ت
ṯ	ṯ	שׁ	ת	ث
š	š	שׁ	שׁ	س
ṭ	ṭ	ט	ט	ط
ṯ (ḏ, ẓ)	ṯ (ḏ)	צ	ט	ظ
ṣ	ṣ	צ	צ	ص
ʿ	ʿ	ע	ע	ع
ḍ	ṣ	צ	ע (ק)	ض
ġ	ġ	ע	ע	غ

Examples:

d: יְדַע "he knew," יַד "hand."

ḏ: דִּכְרָן (Hebrew זִכְרוֹן) "memorandum," דְּבַח (Hebrew זֶבַח) "he sacrificed," מַדְבְּחָא "altar," דְּהַב (Hebrew זָהָב) "gold," אֶדְרָע (Hebrew זְרוֹעַ) "arm," the demonstrative element ד in the pronouns דִּי, דָּא, דְּנָה, and the adverb אֱדַיִן, etc. Note that this sound was originally spelled with ז in Official Aramaic. An original ז sound in a Persian loan word (גִּזְבַּרְיָא "treasurers" E 7:21) was wrongly spelled with ד in D 3:2f. (גְּדָבְרַיָּא).

z: זָיְעִין (וזאעין) "trembling," מָזוֹן "food."

t: בַּיְתָא "house," כְּתַב "he wrote," מַתְּנָן "gifts."

ṯ: תַּמָּה (Hebrew שָׁם) "there," תְּלָת (Hebrew שָׁלוֹשׁ) "three," תּוֹר (Hebrew שׁוֹר) "ox," תְּרַע (Hebrew שַׁעַר, < *taḡr*) "door," יְתִב (Hebrew יָשַׁב) "he sat."

š: רֵאשׁ "head," שְׁמַיָּא "heaven," שְׁאֵל "he asked," שְׁמַע "he heard."

ṭ: טָב "good," טַבָּחַיָּא "butchers, executioners," שַׁלִּיט "mighty," טַל "dew."

ṯ̣: קַיִץ (Hebrew קַיִץ) "summer," תַּטְלֵל (Hebrew צֵל) "seek shade (shelter)," עֵטָא, יָעֲטֹהִי (Hebrew יעץ) "advice, his advisers," טִפְרוֹהִי טִפְרַיָּה (Hebrew צִפֹּרֶן) "his (its) nails," טוּר (Hebrew צוּר) "mountain," נִטְרֵת (Hebrew נצר) "I guarded."

ṣ: צָבֵא "wishing," צְלֵם "image," הַצְלַח "prospered," קַצִּצוּ "cut down!" (pl. masc.).

ʿ: עֲבִידְתָּא "work," עַם "people," יְדַע "he knew," בְּעֵל "master."

ḍ: אַרְעָא (Hebrew אֶרֶץ) "earth," עֲמַר (Hebrew צֶמֶר) "wool," עִלְעִין (Hebrew צֵלָע) "ribs," עָרָיִךְ (Hebrew צָר, צֹרֵר) "your enemies," אָע (< עע, Hebrew עֵץ) "wood," יִמְחֵא (< מחע, Hebrew מחץ) "he hits (stays His hand)," רְעוּת (Hebrew רצה) "wish." In an older stage of Aramaic, Semitic *ḍ* was represented by a sound which was distinct from ע and written ק. This ק is preserved in BA as a historical spelling only in אַרְקָא Jer. 10:11, along with מֵאַרְעָא in the same verse.

ḡ: עַל "he entered," בְּעָא "he desired, requested."

18. Seeming exceptions to these rules require an explanation. Thus, שָׁפְטִין "judges" E 7:25 should be *תפטין; consequently, it cannot be Aramaic but is a loan word from the Canaanite-Hebrew family. זָכוּ "innocence" must be a legal loan word from the Akkadian, because the original root was *ḏkw*. Likewise, שֵׁיצִיא (א) "he completed" E 6:15 must be an Akkadian loan word if only because the Aramaic development of the original root (*wḏ*ʾ, Aramaic *yqʾ*, *yʿʾ*) has ע.

19. שׂ became ס in later Aramaic. In BA times, this process was in its incipient stages. שׂ, in Aramaic words, is as a rule used correctly. Exceptions are סַתְרֵהּ "he tore it down" E 5:12 and, possibly, יִסְבַּר "he intends" D 7:25. Vacillation between שׂ and ס occurs in foreign words, and although this is due to uncertainty concerning the foreign sound, it foreshadows the Aramaic sound change *š > s*: אַרְתַּחְשַׁשְׁתָּא "Artaxerxes" E 4:8, etc., but אַרְתַּחְשַׁסְתְּא E 7:21, כַּשְׂדָּי in D, but כַּסְדָּיֵא "Chaldaean" E 5:12, שַׂבְּכָא "sambuke (harp)" D 3:10, 15, but סַבְּכָא D 3:5, שְׂרֹשִׁי (< שְׁרֹשִׁי, *kᵊṯîḇ* (שרשו) "corporal punishment" E 7:26, corresponding to סרושׁיתא occurring in an Aramaic leather document from Egypt.

20. Consonant doubling in BA involves true gemination; the doubled consonant is pronounced twice with a syllable break in between. Final consonants are not doubled (cf. גֻּבָּא—גֹּב "den," פֻּמֵּהּ—פֻּם "mouth," עַמָּא—עַם "people").

All consonants are capable of gemination except א and ר. The dot indicating gemination is also not used with החע. This suggests that at certain times and in certain areas, החע were also not capable of gemination. But forms with nasalization (הַנְעֵל for *haʿʿēl*) or preceding short vowel (הַעֵלְנִי *haʿʿēlnî* "let me enter" D 2:24f.) confirm the existence of gemination for these consonants.

Short vowels before א and ר are lengthened. In the case of א, the only instance is מֵאַרְעָא "from the earth" Jer. 10:11. For ר, cf., for instance, מְבָרֵךְ (< *mᵊbarrak*) "blessed," תָּרָעַיָּא (< *tarrāʿayyā*) "doorkeepers." Vowel lengthening is also occasionally found before ע, cf. מְרָעַע (< *mᵊraʿʿaʿ*) "breaking" D 2:40, מְסָעֲדִין (< *mᵊsaʿʿᵃḏîn*) "helping" (pl. masc.) E 5:2. The only instance of lengthening before ה: מִתְבָּהַל "disturbed" D 5:9 is doubtful, and gemination, as usual in the case of החע, seems preferable.

21. Substitution of nasalization for gemination is frequently found: תִּנְדַּע (< *tiddaʿ*) "you will know" E 4:15, מַנְדַּע (< *maddaʿ*)

"knowledge," לְהַנְסָקָה "to bring up," next to הֻסַּק "he was brought up," D 6:24.

Where original *n* appears unassimilated, secondary nasalization, instead of retention of the original sound, may be involved.

22. Original long vowels have been retained throughout. This applies also to *ā*, which became *ọ̄* in Hebrew at an early period: טָב (Hebrew טוב) "good," תְּלָת (Hebrew שָׁלוֹשׁ) "three."

אֱנָשָׁא (ⁱᵃ*nọ̄šā*, read ⁱᵃ*nāšā*, the common form) "mankind" is not a Hebraism, but originated through vowel assimilation from *ⁱᵃ*unāš* (cf. תְּחוֹת *tuḥāt* "underneath"). The suffixed element *-ọ̄n* is found in noun formations in addition to *-ān*: דִּכְרוֹנָה E 6:2 and דִּכְרָנְיָא "memorandum," שִׁלְטֹנֵי "officials" D 3:2f., and שָׁלְטָן "rule," רַעְיוֹנִי (in Bab. vocalization *riʿyọ̄n-*) "my thoughts." עֶלְיוֹנִין "most high," on the other hand, is a Hebraism (par. 187). מְדָר- and -מְדוֹר "dwelling" are different noun formations.

23. Short vowels in unstressed open syllables have been reduced to a zero or murmured vowel. Inversely, preservation of a short vowel in an open syllable usually requires that that syllable be stressed. Cf., for instance, תְּלָת (*tᵉlāṯ < ṯalāṯ*, Hebrew שָׁלוֹשׁ with pretone lengthening) "three," כְּתַבוּ (*kᵉṯábū < katabū*, Hebrew כָּתְבוּ *kā̇ṯᵉḇú*) "they wrote," סְלִקוּ (*sᵉliqū < saliqū*) "they went up." For בְּטֵלַת, cf. par. 10.

In some cases, short *a* was retained in pronunciation and became lengthened secondarily: מָרִים "raising up" D 5:19, יְהָקִים "he sets up" D 5:21, 6:16 (par. 141). Cf. also מָזוֹן "food."

Note the strange absence of the gemination of מ in חַרְטֻמַיָּא "magicians" D 4:4, 6, and אֻמַיָּא "nations" D 3:4 (but אֻמַּיָּא E 4:10).

24. Short *i/ę* before החער closing a syllable becomes *a*: אֲמַר "saying" (but שְׁאֵל "asking"), מְשַׁבַּח "praising" (but מְמַלֵּל "speaking"). In verbs ending in החער, this process extends to open syllables (par. 115).

25. Occasional pausal lengthening of short vowels is admitted in Tiberian vocalization: חָיִל "strength" E 4:23, D 3:4, יְדָי "my hands" D 3:15, קְדָמָי (< *qᵒdāmay*) "before me" D 2:6, שָׁמְרָיִן (< *Šā̇mᵉráyin*) "Samaria" E 4:10, 17, עֲנָיִן (< *ᶜᵃnáyin*) "humble, poor" D 4:24.

26. The main word stress falls usually on the last syllable.

Penult stress occurs in certain grammatical formations where the suffixed element has a long vowel. This applies to:

(1) independent personal pronouns (par. 29): אֲנַחְנָה "we" (but *ʾắnắ, himmố*).

(2) pronominal suffixes (par. 31): הַעֵלְנִי "let me enter!" אֲבֹוּהִי "his father," הַקְרְבֹוּהִי "they brought him near," עֲלֹוהִי "upon him," אֲבָהָתְנָא "our fathers," etc. However, the suffix of the 1. sg. in connection with nouns and prepositions is always stressed, except in אָבִי "my father" D 5:13.

(3) suffixed elements of the verb: יְדַעְתָּ "you knew," כְּתַבוּ "they wrote," שְׁאֵלְנָא "we asked," אֲכֻלִי "eat!" (sg. fem.), שְׁבֻקוּ "leave!" (pl. masc.), יֵאבַדוּ "let them perish!" (par. 108), etc. Exceptions are the endings of verbs originally having או as their last consonant wherever these endings result from contraction (*-ố < -áyū*, etc., par. 145ff.).

(4) the adverbial ending *-ā* (par. 88), including אָסְפַּרְנָא (*ʾospárnā*) "exactly," כֹּלָּא (*kόllā*) "totally."

Penult stress further occurs where the vowel of the last syllable merely serves the purpose of dissolving a consonant cluster: אֶבֶן (< *ʾabn*) "stone," קַיְט "summer," and equivalent noun formations (par. 51); יְדָיִן "hands" and other duals (par. 45); הַשְׁכַּחַת "I found," סָפַת "it (fem.) ceased," and similar verbal forms (par. 117). Also דָּרְיָוֶשׁ (*Dắrᵊyắweš*) "Darius," כֹּורֶשׁ "Cyrus," but בָּבֶל (*Bāḇḗl*) "Babylon."

Exceptional cases of penult stress are כְּנֵמָא "thus," מֶנִּי "appoint!" (par. 153), אֵלֶּה "these" (par. 32).

27. Enclitic use of the prepositions ל and ב, or of a genitive, may deprive a word of its stress or result in an exceptional stress (principal or secondary) on the penult: וְיֵאמַר לֵהּ (*wᵊyḗmarlẹh*) "and says to Him" D 4:32, הוּסְפַת לִי (*hûsᵊp̄aṭlí*) "was given to me in addition" D 4:33, מִתְעֲבֵד בַּהּ (*mitᶜᵃḇedbáh*) "being done in it" E 4:19, גֻּבְרֵי חַיִל (*gibbắrẹ̄-ḥáyil*) "strongmen" D 3:20, בְּסְפַר דָּכְרָנַיָּא (*bisᵊp̄ar-doḵrắnayyắ*) "in the record book" E 4:15.

28. Secondary stress occurs in words of more than two syllables. In the Biblical text, it is often indicated by a short vertical line to the left of the vowel sign (ֽ◌, ◌ֽ , etc.). Where this line occurs to the right of the vowel sign (◌ֽ), it was added by the editors of the "Kittel Bible" but is not found in the manuscripts.

In transliteration, ◌́ indicates the main stress, ◌̀ the secondary stress.

IV. The Pronoun

29. Independent personal pronouns:

	sg.		pl.
I	אֲנָה	we	אֲנַ֫חְנָה
you (masc.)	אַנְתְּ, אַנְתָּה	you (masc.)	אַנְתּוּן, *אַנְתֹּם
	(ʾántā, read ʾant)		
you (fem.)	*אַנְתִּי	you (fem.)	**אַנְתֵּן
he	הוּא	they (masc.)	אִנּוּן, הִמּוֹן, הִמּוֹ
she	הִיא	they (fem.)	אִנִּין

The spelling אֲנַ֫חְנָא is found in E 5:11, אַנְתְּ in E 7:25.

הִמּוֹ occurs in E, הִמּוֹן in D. With one exception (אֲנַ֫חְנָא הִמּוֹ עַבְדֹ֫והִי "we are His servants" E 5:11), both הִמּוֹ and הִמּוֹן happen to be used as direct objects immediately following a verb in the perfect tense.

30. The pronouns of the third person may be used as the copula, even where the subject of the sentence is a pronoun of the first or second person: דִּי הוּא אֱלָהָא חַיָּא "who is the living God" D 6:27, דִּי הִיא שְׁנַת "which is the year . . ." E 6:15, חֲדָה הִיא דָתְכוֹן "one (and the same) is the law applicable to you" D 2:9, הֲלָא דָא הִיא בָּבֶל "is this not Babylon?" D 4:27, דִּי אִנִּין אַרְבַּע "which are four" D 7:17, אַנְתָּה הוּא "we are His servants" E 5:11, אַנְתָּה הוּא רֵאשָׁה דִּי דַהֲבָא "you are the head of gold" D 2:38, אַנְתָּה הוּא דָנִיֵּאל "you are Daniel?" D 5:13, מַן אִנּוּן שְׁמָהָת גֻּבְרַיָּא "what (par. 38) are the names of the men?" E 5:4. The only example of an indetermined predicate is וּמַן הוּא אֱלָהּ דִּי "and who is a god who . . ." D 3:15.

31. Pronominal suffixes: In addition to the independent personal pronouns, BA has pronominal suffixes that may be added to nouns (par. 49, cf. also par. 95), prepositions (par. 77 ff.), and verbs (par. 174 ff.). In connection with nouns, these suffixes represent possessive pronouns, and in connection with prepositions and verbs, the objective case of the independent personal pronoun.

The basic forms are:

	sg.	pl.
1.	־ִי (־ִני with verbs)	־ָנָא
2. masc.	־ָךְ	־כֹם, ־כוֹן
2. fem.	־כִי*	־כֵן**
3. masc.	־ה (-eh), ־הִי (after long vowels)	־הֹם, ־הוֹן
3. fem.	־ה (-ah)	־הֵן (keṯib הֵן-)

The 3. pl. suffix is not used with verbs (cf. par. 174).

An independent objective pronoun, formed by *יָת with suffix, occurs in BA only once: יָתְהוֹן "them" D 3:12.

An independent possessive pronoun is formed by the relative pronoun דִּי followed by the preposition ל: חָכְמְתָא וּגְבוּרְתָא דִּי לֵהּ הִיא "wisdom and power are His" D 2:20.

32. Demonstrative pronouns:

	sg.		pl.	
masc.	דְּנָה	masc./fem.	אִלֵּין (אֵלֶּה ,אֵלֶּה)
fem.	דָּא		
masc.	דֵּךְ		אִלֵּךְ
fem.	דָּךְ		
masc.	דִּכֵּן		
fem.	דִּכֵּן		
masc.	הוּא		אִנּוּן

אֵלֶּה (elle) occurs in Jer. 10:11, אֵלֶּה (read el) in E 5:15.

אִלֵּךְ occurs only as masc., but the fem. can be assumed to be identical in form.

For הוּא and אִנּוּן (independent personal pronouns used as demonstrative pronouns), cf. הוּא צַלְמָא "that image" D 2:32 and מַלְכַיָּא אִנּוּן "those kings" D 2:44.

After prepositions, BA knows a demonstrative element ה that is assimilated to the pronominal suffixes (par. 89).

33. The demonstrative pronoun can be used as a noun: עַל דְּנָה "concerning this," כִּדְנָה, לָקֳבֵל דְּנָה "in accordance with this, thus," דְּנָה הוּא "this is it" D 2:28, דָּא לְדָא "the one ... the other" D 5:6, דָּא מִן דָּא "the one from the other" D 7:3. Cf., in particular, the use of the masc. with reference to a fem. noun: מִלָּה כִדְנָה "a matter like this" D 2:10.

34. Used as an adjective, the demonstrative pronoun usually follows the noun to which it belongs. This noun must have the definite article or an equivalent form of determination, i. e., it must be in the construct state (par. 48), or have a pronominal suffix, or be a proper name.

Cases of demonstrative pronouns preceding the noun are: דְּנָה בִּנְיָנָא "this building" E 5:4, אֵלֶּה מָאנַיָּא "these vessels" E 5:15, הוּא צַלְמָא "that image" D 2:32, דְּנָה חֶלְמָא "this dream" D 4:15, אִלֵּין חֵיוָתָא "these animals" D 7:17.

35. The relative pronoun is דִּי. It is used for all genders and numbers.

The form דְּ (< דִּי), which is common in later Aramaic, occurs in the misreading דְּהַוָא (*Dehhāyē*) E 4:9, for דִּי הוּא "that is".

For further uses of דִּי, cf. par. 86.

36. As דִּי cannot be declined, oblique cases must be indicated by pronominal suffixes attached to appropriate components of the relative clause. Cf. אַנְתָּה ... דִּי אֱלָהּ שְׁמַיָּא ... יְהַב לָךְ "you ... to whom the God of Heaven gave" D 2:37, דִּי כָל מַעֲבָדוֹהִי קְשֹׁט "all of whose works are as they should be" D 4:34, דִּי מַלְכָּא שָׂם שְׁמֵהּ בֵּלְטְשַׁאצַּר "whose name the king had made Belteshazzar" D 5:12, דִּי נִשְׁמְתָךְ בִּידֵהּ "in Whose hand your soul is" D 5:23.

The direct object case, however, is only rarely indicated in this or any other manner. Examples for the direct object relationship expressed by a pronominal suffix are: דִּי פֶחָה שָׂמֵהּ "whom he had made governor" E 5:14, דִּי אֲנָה בֱנֵיתַהּ לְבֵית מַלְכוּ "which I have built for a royal capital" D 4:27, דִּי אַנְתָּה פָּלַח לֵהּ "whom (par. 182) you worship" D 6:17, 21.

37. The indefinite relative pronouns are:

מַן דִּי "whoever"

מָה, מָה דִּי "whatever."

Simple דִּי "whatever (whomever)" is found in D 5:19.

38. The interrogative pronouns are:

מַן "who?"

מָה "what?"

The use of מָ in E 5:4, מַן אִנּוּן שְׁמָהָת גֻּבְרַיָּא "what(!) are the names of the men?", reflects the thought: "who are the men?".

V. The Noun and the Adjective

39. Nouns and adjectives, unless they are of non-Semitic origin, may be classified as belonging to "roots" composed of two or, in most cases, three consonants (or "radicals"). They may be further classified according to modifications that the root may undergo through (1) the use of various short or long vowels following the radicals, (2) the gemination of the second or third consonant, or (3) the addition of prefixed (י-, m-, t-) or suffixed (-ān, -ōn, -īt, -ūt, -āy) elements. Instead of gemination of the second or third consonant, one also finds reduplication of a two-consonant root (הַרְהֹרִין "imaginings") or of the last two consonants of a three-consonant root (שְׁפַרְפָּרָא "dawn"). In BA, all words of four or more consonants are of foreign origin either as recent loan words or as ancient cultural terms (as, for instance, פַּרְזֶל "iron").

As a convenient mode of reference, grammarians have chosen one particular root, such as p⁽l (qtl, ktb), to indicate a given nominal or adjectival formation, for instance, pa⁽l, p⁽āl, mip⁽al, p⁽al⁽āl, etc.

40. Some nominal and adjectival formations have come to be associated with certain categories of meaning. Thus, p⁽īl and pa⁽⁽īl are widely used for adjectives (דְּחִיל "frightful," שַׁלִּיט "mighty," חַכִּים "wise"). Pa⁽⁽āl is used to indicate professional status (דַּיָּנִין "judges," טַבָּחַיָּא "butchers, executioners," זַמָּרַיָּא "musicians," תָּרָעַיָּא "doorkeepers"), and so is *pāʿōl*, represented by כָּרוֹזָא "herald." The preformative *ma-*, *mi-* often indicates locality (*מִשְׁתְּא "place where one drinks, banquet"). The suffixes *-īṯ*, *-ūṯ* (par. 56f.) have come to denote abstract meaning (מַלְכָּא "king," מַלְכוּתָא "kingship, kingdom"). The "gentilic" ending *-āy* (par. 58) indicates belonging to something.

41. Nouns have two genders, masc. and fem.; three numbers, sg., pl., and dual; and three "states," corresponding to the form without the definite article ("absolute state" = *abs. st.*), the form used before a depending noun that is in the position of our genitive ("construct state" = *cstr. st.*), and the form with the definite article ("determined state" = *det. st.*).

There is no formal distinction between nouns and adjectives. Adjectives are placed after the nouns to which they belong and to which they conform grammatically as closely as possible.

42. Nouns and adjectives are declined as follows:

	masc. sg.		fem. sg.
abs. st.	טָב	"good"	טָבָה
cstr. st.	טָב		טָבַת
det. st.	טָבָא		טָבְתָא

	masc. pl.	fem. pl.
abs. st.	טָבִין	טָבָן
cstr. st.	טָבֵי	טָבָת
det. st.	טָבַיָּא (יְהוּדָיֵא)	טָבָתָא

Formations with the gentilic ending *-āy* (par. 58) have *-ē̦*, instead of *-ayyā*, in the det. st. of the pl. masc.

The original spelling of the postpositive article is א-, but instances of a spelling with -ה occur, in particular in connection with the sg. masc.

The original spelling of the ending of the abs. st. fem. is ה-, but sporadic examples of spellings with א- occur.

For irregular non-spirantization of the ending of the det. st. of the sg. fem., cf. above, par. 15.

יִם_, instead of יִן_, as the ending of the abs. st. of the pl. masc.
(מְלָכִים "kings" E 4:13, אֲנָשִׁים "men" D 4:14, אַלְפִים "thousands"
D 7:10), is a Hebraism.

43. The definite article is a demonstrative element. Therefore, it
can also serve to indicate the vocative: מַלְכָּא לְעָלְמִין חֱיִי "O king,
live for ever!" For the ending -*ā* as a remnant of an ancient accusative, cf. par. 88.

44. The fem. is used to form nouns from adjectives: שְׁחִיתָה
"corruption" D 6:5, עֲמִיקָתָא וּמְסַתְּרָתָא "deep and hidden matters"
D 2:22, חַשְׁחָן "needed things" E 6:9, רַבְרְבָן "big words" D 7:8.

45. The dual is preserved only in remnants. It is used with parts
of the body that occur in pairs in nature: יְדָיִן "hands", רַגְלַיִן "feet,"
שִׁנַּיִן "two (rows of) teeth" D 7:7. In such nouns, the dual may be
used for the pl.: קַרְנַיִן עֲשַׂר "ten horns" D 7:7. Further duals are
מָאתַיִן "two hundred" and תְּרֵי (cstr. st. masc.), תַּרְתֵּין (fem.)
"two."

All other forms of the dual of the masc. noun, including those
with pronominal suffixes, are identical with the pl. forms and not
distinguishable from them. No dual of a fem. formation or of an
adjective is found.

46. Use of the abs. st. and the det. st. agrees by and large with
the non-use or use of the definite article in English. The det. st.
may also be used for the general designation of species: חֲמְרָא שָׁתֵה
"he was drinking *wine*" D 5:1, מָאנַיָּא דִי בֵית אֱלָהָא דִּי דַהֲבָה וְכַסְפָּא
"the vessels of *gold* and *silver* belonging to the house of God"
E 5:14.

The numeral חד "one" is used occasionally to denote indeter-
mination in the sg.: אִגְּרָה חֲדָה "a letter" E 4:8, מְגִלָּה חֲדָה "a scroll"
E 6:2, צְלֵם חַד "an image" D 2:31, שָׁעָה חֲדָה "an hour (a while)"
D 4:16, אֶבֶן חֲדָה "a stone" D 6:18, שְׂטַר חַד "one side" D 7:5.

Note in the following enumeration how the nouns of Greek origin,
in contrast to the Aramaic ones, are left without the definite
article: קָל קַרְנָא מַשְׁרוֹקִיתָא קִיתָרוֹס סַבְּכָא פְּסַנְתֵּרִין סוּמְפֹּנְיָה וְכֹל זְנֵי זְמָרָא
"the sound of the horn, pipe, *zither*, sambuke (harp), *psaltery*,
symphony (bagpipe?), and all kinds of music(al instruments)"
D 3:5, 7, 10, 15.

47. The cstr. st. implies determination: מִלַּת מַלְכָּא "*the* word of the king."

Indetermination of the first element of a genitive construction must be expressed by some sort of circumlocution: מֶלֶךְ לְיִשְׂרָאֵל רַב "*a* great king of Israel" E 5:11.

We call the second element "genitive" because it is found in positions where Semitic and Indo-European languages that have preserved case endings use the genitive. If this genitive is in the abs. st., the entire construction may seemingly be indetermined, as in עֲנַשׁ נִכְסִין "a property fine" E 7:26, בַּר אֱלָהִין "a divine being" D 3:25.

The cstr. st. may be used before a prepositional expression: מַלְכְוָת תְּחוֹת כָּל שְׁמַיָּא "the kingdoms underneath the entire heaven" D 7:27. But, in general, nothing can come between a cstr. st. and its depending genitive. Thus, demonstrative pronouns referring to the noun in the cstr. st. follow at the end: בֵּית אֱלָהָא דְנָה "this house of God".

It is possible for more than one genitive to depend upon a single noun in the cstr. st.: מִלֵּי מַלְכָּא וְרַבְרְבָנוֹהִי "the words of the king and his magnates" D 5:10, etc.

48. The cstr. st. is the basic form for expression of the genitive relationship. However, there are altogether three different ways to express a genitive construction in BA:

(a)	בֵּית אֱלָהָא	"the house of God"
(b)	בֵּיתָא דִי אֱלָהָא	
(c)	בֵּיתֵהּ דִי אֱלָהָא	
(a)	שְׁמָהָת גֻּבְרַיָּא	"the names of the men"
(b)	שְׁמָהָתָא דִי גֻבְרַיָּא	
(c)	שְׁמָהָתְהוֹן דִי גֻבְרַיָּא	

The use of the cstr. st. is preponderant in BA. Construction (c), with proleptic pronominal suffix, is comparatively rare. The intermediate form (b) appears to have come into use originally in order to break up long strings of successive genitives but in BA, it is used indiscriminately alongside the cstr. st. Cf., for instance, עֲבִידְתָּא דִי מְדִינַת בָּבֶל "the administration of the Province of Babylon" D 2:49, but עֲבִידַת מְדִינַת בָּבֶל D 3:12, גֹּב אַרְיָוָתָא "the lions' den" D 6:8, 13, 25, but גֻּבָּא דִי אַרְיָוָתָא D 6:17, 20.

3*

49. The noun with pronominal suffixes:

masc. sg.		fem. sg.	
אֱלָהִי	"my god"	חֵיוְתִי	"my animal"
אֱלָהָךְ	"your" (masc.)	חֵיוְתָךְ	
אֱלָהֵכִי*	"your" (fem.)	חֵיוְתֵכִי*	
אֱלָהֵהּ	"his"	חֵיוְתֵהּ	
אֱלָהַהּ	"her"	חֵיוְתַהּ*	
אֱלָהַנָא	"our"	חֵיוְתַנָא*	
אֱלָהֲכֹם (-כֹן)	"your" (masc.)	חֵיוְתְכֹם (-כֹן)*	
אֱלָהֲכֵן**	"your" (fem.)	חֵיוְתְכֵן**	
אֱלָהֲהֹם (-הֹן)	"their" (masc.)	חֵיוְתְהֹם (-הֹן)*	
אֱלָהֲהֵן	"their" (fem.)	חֵיוְתְהֵן**	

masc. pl.		fem. pl.	
אֱלָהַי	"my gods"	חֵיוְתִי	"my animals"
אֱלָהָיךְ	"your" (masc.)	חֵיוְתָךְ	
אֱלָהָיכִי*	"your" (fem.)	חֵיוְתֵכִי*	
אֱלָהֹוהִי	"his"	חֵיוְתֵהּ	
אֱלָהֶיהַ	"her"	חֵיוְתַהּ	
אֱלָהֵינָא	"our"	חֵיוְתַנָא	
אֱלָהֵיכֹם (-כֹן)	"your" (masc.)	חֵיוְתְכֹם (-כֹן)*	
אֱלָהֵיכֵן**	"your" (fem.)	חֵיוְתְכֵן**	
אֱלָהֵיהֹם (-הֹן)	"their" (masc.)	חֵיוְתְהֹם (-הֹן)	
אֱלָהֵיהֵן	"their" (fem.)	חֵיוְתְהֵן**	

Note the kᵉṯīḇ-qᵉrē distinction in the pl. of the masc. noun:
אֱלָהָיךְ (ᵉlāhāḵ), אֱלָהֵיהַ (ᵉlāhah), אֱלָהֵינָא (ᵉlāhánā).
The vowel preceding the suffix of the 1. pl. is variously given.
Thus, we find אֱלָהֳנָא "our god" D 3:17, אֲבָהָתֳנָא "our fathers"
E 5:12, לְשֵׁיזָבוּתֳנָא "to save us" D 3:17, אִיתָינָא "we are" D 3:18,
לֶנָא "for us" E 4:14, עֲלֶינָא "to us" E 4:12, 18, 5:17. The evidence
strongly favors short stressed a (> e in ᶜaléna).

The suffix of the 3. pl. fem. is written like the corresponding masc.
form: כֻּלְּהֵן "all of them" D 7:19, בֵּינֵיהֵן "between them" D 7:8.

50. Wherever the final consonant of the root is preceded by a long vowel, no changes in the vocalization of the word are required by the declension or by the addition of the pronominal suffixes.

In other noun formations, minor changes in the vocalization may result, among which the following may be noted:

51. *Pacl, picl, pucl* (and corresponding fem. forms): The abs. and cstr. st. of the masc. becomes *pᵊca/e/ol*.

For original *pacl*, cf. כְּסַף "silver," אֲלַף "thousand," תְּלַג "snow," חֲמַר "wine," גְּבַר "man" (pl. גֻּבְרִין, Bab. vocalization *gaḇrin*), טְעֵם "order," צְלֵם "image," עֲבֵד "slave," בְּעֵל "master." In לְחֶם "meal, banquet" D 5:1, the unusual e (ms. variant reading with ẹ) may represent a. Whenever an ending is added, we find the original form: כַּסְפָּא, אַלְפָּא, טַעְמָא, מַלְכְּתָא "queen," etc., but also שִׁמְשָׁא "sun."

For original *picl*, cf. פְּשַׁר "interpretation," סְפַר "book," מְלַח "salt." With endings, we find פִּשְׁרָא, סִפְרִין, מִלְכִּי "my advice," חֶלְמָא "dream," גְּשְׁמְהוֹן "their body," בִּקְעַת "plain" (cstr. st.).

For original *pucl*, cf. קְשֹׁט "truth," כְּתַל "wall" D 5:5 (pl. כֻּתְלַיָּא E 5:8), and, presumably, רְגַז "wrath" and תְּקָף (*tᵊqop*, Bab. vocalization *tᵊqoḇ*, par. 10) "strength." With endings, o is the preferred vowel: תָּקְפָּא "strength", נֻגְהָא "dawn," שָׁרְשׁוֹהִי "its roots," עָפְיֵהּ "its foliage," חָכְמְתָא, חָכְמָה "wisdom," אָרְחָתֵהּ "His ways," but כֻּתְלַיָּא "the walls."

However, these noun formations have another abs. and cstr. st. with anaptyctic vowel after the second consonant (*pécel, pécel* [*pácal*, on account of the laryngal]). This is the accepted form in Hebrew. Cf. מֶלֶךְ "king," קֶרֶן "horn," צֶלֶם "image," אֶלֶף "thousand," חֵלֶם "dream," טַעַם "order," and, in a loan word, פַּרְשֶׁגֶן "copy."

The original pl. formation of *pa/i/ucl* was **pa/i/ucalīn*, with an a vowel in the second syllable. This vowel has left a trace in the preserved spirantization of following בגדכפת: מַלְכִין "kings," עֲבְדוֹהִי "his slaves," but נִסְכֵּיהוֹן "their libations" E 7:17. יַרְכָתֵהּ "its thighs" may be rather a *pacil* formation.

In roots with y as the second consonant, we always find the form with the anaptyctic vowel in the abs. st.: קַיְט "summer," חַיְל "strength." In the cstr. st., the original diphthong is contracted: בֵּית "house," חֵיל "army," עֵין "eye." In all other forms, the diphthong is preserved; in D 4:1, the variant reading בֵּיתִי, "my house" is preferable to the accepted form בֵּיתִי.

52. Word formations with two short vowels (*paᶜal*, etc.). Their declension is governed by the rule of the disappearance of short unstressed vowels in open syllables (par. 23): דְּהַב, דַּהֲבָא (with *b̲*) "gold," אֲתַר, אֲתָרֵה, אַתְרָה "place," חַבְרוֹהִי "his companions," בְּשַׂר, בִּשְׂרָא "flesh, mankind," זְמַן, זִמְנָא "time." The *i* vowel in the last two cases is secondary (*a > i*).

53. Word formations with a long and a short vowel are also governed by the same rule: אָשַׁף, אָשְׁפִין "enchanter," עָלַם, עָלְמִין "eternity."

54. Words ending in *-y*, such as *פְּתִי*, פְּתָיֵהּ "its breadth," show no irregularities.

חֲדוֹהִי "its breast," מְעוֹהִי "its belly" D 2:32 appear to belong to *חֲדֶה*, מְעָה, forming a dual/plural *חֲדַיִן*, מְעַיִן (cf. the participles בְּנֵה, בְּנַיִן, par. 150). However, a number of words ending in *-y*, such as כֻּרְסָא (*korsē̦*) "chair," אַרְיֵה "lion," לֵילְיָא "night" (det. st.), with suffix כֻּרְסְיֵהּ "his chair," have the pl. כָּרְסָן, *כֻּרְסָוָת*, כֻּרְסָוָתָא, אַרְיָוָתָא.

מָרֵא "lord, master" presupposes a form where final א has become *y* (det. st. *מָרְיָא*), rather than an original *māriᵞ*. However, "my lord" is מָרִי (*māri < mārᵊᵞi*).

55. In word formations of roots with final *w*, *w* is retained in the one masc. formation *חֵזוּ*, חֶזְוָא "vision." In fem. formations, there are three possibilities: (1) *w* may be retained as in חֶדְוָה "joy." (2) It may become *ō*, as in חֲזוֹתַהּ "its appearance." But (3) in most cases, it becomes *ū*, as in רְבוּ "greatness," צְבוּ "(some)-thing," שְׁלוּ "neglect," בָּעוּ "request," cstr. st. רְעוּת "wish," with the definite article or pronominal suffixes רְבוּתֶךָ, רְבוּתָא, גָּלוּתָא "exile," בָּעוּתֵהּ. This formation has become indistinguishable from the abstract ending *-ūṯ*. In fact, in some of these words, the original root ended in *y*, and the preponderance of *ū* is due to the influence of the abstract ending.

56. Nouns with the abstract ending *-ūṯ*: Abs. st. מַלְכוּ "king-dom," בְּהִילוּ "haste," נְהִירוּ "brilliance," שָׂכְלְתָנוּ "intelligence." Cstr. st. מַלְכוּת, חַשְׁחוּת "needs." Det. st. מַלְכוּתָא, שָׂהֲדוּתָא "testimony." With suffix מַלְכוּתִי.

The pl. is *מַלְכָן*, מַלְכְוָת, מַלְכְוָתָא.

57. The endings -*i*, -*it*: Long -*i* serves as a fem. ending in אֵימְתָנִי (-*ān-i*) "frightful." In אָחֳרִי (*oḥᵒri*) "other" (fem. of אָחֳרָן), it may go back to an original ending -*ay* > -*ẹ̄*.

The abstract ending has the abs. st. -*i*, cstr. st. -*it*, det. st. -*itā*, pl. *-ᵊyān*, etc. It is sparsely represented: שְׁרֹשִׁי (*kᵊtib* שרשו) "corporal punishment" E 7:26 (where the ending *y* belonged to the original Persian word but was interpreted as the Aramaic formative, cf. par. 19, 189), אַחֲרִית "end" D 2:28, אַרְעִית "bottom" D 6:25, מַשְׁרוֹקִיתָא "pipe" D 3:5, 7, 10, 15, עֲלִיתֵהּ "its upper room" D 6:11; נְוָלִי "dunghill" D 2:5, 3:29 (but נְוָלוּ E 6:11) is of uncertain origin and formation (par. 190) but seems to have been adapted to this class of nouns.

58. The ending -*āy* (gentilic formations and ordinal numbers): The det. st. of the pl. ends in -*ẹ̄*, cf. יְהוּדָיֵא "Jews," בָּבְלָיֵא "Babylonians," כַּשְׂדָּיֵא (*Kaśdāyẹ̄*) "Chaldaeans."

Between the *ā* and another vowel, *y* is frequently replaced by the glottal stop (par. 14), which occasionally appears also expressed in writing: כַּשְׂדָּאִין D 3:8, יְהוּדָאִין (*Yᵊhūdā᾽in*, read *Yᵊhūdāyin*!) D 3:12.

In certain foreign words, such as אֲפַרְסַתְכָיֵא "magistrates" (?) E 4:9, תִּפְתָּיֵא "police chiefs," addition of the ending -*āy* seems erroneous in view of their meaning and origin.

59. Nouns without the fem. ending may nevertheless be fem. in gender. Such nouns are parts of the body that occur in pairs: יַד "hand," *רְגַל "foot," עַיִן "eye," קֶרֶן "horn," שִׁנַּיִן ... רַבְרְבָן "two big (rows of) teeth" D 7:7. Other parts of the body that are fem. in gender are תְּלָת עִלְעִין "three ribs" D 7:5, גַּפִּין אַרְבַּע "four wings" D 7:6 (but masc. D 7:4). *אֶצְבַּע "finger" has the fem. pl. ending, אֶצְבְּעָן.

Further fem. nouns are אֶבֶן "stone," *אֲרַע "earth," *צִפַּר "bird" (D 4:18, but in D 4:9, the *kᵊtib* of the verb, יְדֻרָן צִפֲּרֵי שְׁמַיָּא "the birds of heaven dwell," is masc.), דָּת (a Persian loan word where the final *t* may have suggested the fem. gender). Others, such as עִזִּין "(she) goats," are fem., though the grammatical gender is not apparent in BA.

רוּחַ "spirit, wind" is usually fem., but masc. in D 2:35. Likewise, נוּר "fire," fem. in D 3:6, etc., is used as masc. in D 3:27, 7:9. Cf. also רֵיחַ נוּר לָא עֲדָת "the smell of fire did not come forth" D 3:27, where the fem. form of the verb may refer to "fire" rather than "smell"; a Dead Sea (Qumrān) variant reads the masc. עדה.

Names of cities and countries may be fem.: בָּבֶל רַבְּתָא "Babylon the great" D 4:27.

60. Masc. sg. formations may have the ending of the fem. pl. Cf. par. 54 and 62, also אֶצְבְּעָן (fem.) "fingers" and אׇרְחָתֵהּ (presumably fem.) "His ways."

61. Fem. sg. formations taking the masc. ending in the pl. are מִלָּה "word" (מִלַּיָּא רַבְרְבָתָא "the big words" D 7:11), *שְׁנָה "year" (שְׁנִין שַׂגִּיאָן "many years" E 5:11), אֻמָּה, pl. אֻמַּיָּא "nation." There are more such nouns of which forms of the sg. are not found in BA: *כַּוָּה (כַּוִּין פְּתִיחָן "open windows" D 6:11), *אַמָּה (אַמִּין "cubits"), *חִנְטָה (חִנְטִין "wheat").

62. Some irregular nouns and adjectives:

*אַב "father" shows long ū before pronominal suffixes, except that of the 1. sg.

(ʾábī) אָבִי	*אֲבוּנָא
אֲבוּךְ	*אֲבוּכֹם (-כֹון)
*אֲבוּכִי	*אֲבוּכֶן
אֲבוּהִי	*אֲבוּהֹם (-הֹון)
*אֲבוּהּ	*אֲבוּהֶן

The pl. is *אֲבָהָן, אֲבָהָתִי, אֲבָהָתָךְ, אֲבָהָתָנָא.

*אַח "brother" does not occur in the sg. with suffixes where its forms would correspond to those of *אַב (*אֲחוּךְ, etc.). The pl. is *אַחִין (ʾaḥḥin), אֲחָיךְ (ʾeḥḥāk) "your colleagues" E 7:18.

*אַנְתָּה "woman, wife" is represented by the pl. *נָשִׁין, נְשֵׁיהֹן D 6:25, from another root.

*בַּיִת "house" (par. 51) has the pl. *בָּתִּין, בָּתֵּיכֹון D 2:5. The pronunciation is problematic, probably bātēkōn, with exceptional non-spirantization of the t.

בַּר "son," with suffix בְּרֵהּ, has the pl. *בְּנִין, בְּנֵי, בְּנֹוהִי, בְּנֵיהֹון.

יֹום "day" has the regular pl. יֹומִין, but יֹומָת עָלְמָא "days of eternity" E 4:15, 19.

*כְּנָה (*כְּנָת?) "colleague" has the pl. *כְּנָן, כְּנָתֵהּ, כְּנָוָתְהֹון.

מָרֵא "lord," see par. 54.

נִבְזְבָּה "gift" D 2:6 appears in a pl. formation נְבִזְבְּיָתָךְ D 5:17.
עַם, עַמָּא "people" has the pl. עַמְמַיָּא (< ʿamamayyā, cf. מַלְכִין
< malaḵīn, par. 51).

פֶּחָה (peḥḥā), cstr. st. פַּחַת (paḥḥaṯ), "governor" has the pl. פֶּחֲוָתָא.
בְּקִרְיָה דִי: קִרְיָה (קִרְיָא E 4:15), קִרְיְתָא "city" has a pl. det. st. קִרְיָה
שָׁמְרָיִן "in the towns of Samaria" E 4:10.

רֵאשׁ "head" forms the pl. רָאשֵׁיהֹם E 5:10 (as in Hebrew), but also
has the normal Aramaic form רֵאשִׁין D 7:6.

רַב, רַבָּא "great, big" forms its pl. with reduplication: רַבְרְבִין,
רַבְרְבָן. Used as a noun meaning "chief, magnate," this pl. is further
augmented by the ending -ān: רַבְרְבָנִי, *רַבְרְבָנִין etc.

רִבּוֹ "myriad" has the pl. רִבְוָן, i. e., ribbʳwān, but the qʳrē is
ribʳbān.

שֵׁם "name", with suffix שְׁמֵהּ, has the pl. שְׁמָהַת, *שְׁמָהָן, שְׁמָהַתְהֹם, שְׁמָהָתְהֹם.
שָׁעָה "hour, while," but בַּהּ שַׁעֲתָא "at once" (par. 89).

VI. Numerals

63. Cardinal numbers:

	masc.	fem.
1	חַד	חֲדָה
2	*תְּרֵין	תַּרְתֵּין
3	תְּלָתָה	תְּלָת
4	אַרְבְּעָה	אַרְבַּע
5	*חַמְשָׁה	*חֲמֵשׁ
6	*שִׁתָּה	שֵׁת (שֵׁת)
7	שִׁבְעָה	*שְׁבַע
8	*תְּמַנְיָה	*תְּמָנֶה
9	*תִּשְׁעָה	*תְּשַׁע
10	עֲשַׂרָה	עֲשַׂר
12	תְּרֵי עֲשַׂר	
20		עֶשְׂרִין
30		תְּלָתִין
40		*אַרְבְּעִין
50		*חַמְשִׁין

60	שִׁתִּין
70	שִׁבְעִין*
80	תְּמָנִין*
90	תִּשְׁעִין*
100	מְאָה
200	מָאתַ֫יִן
400	אַרְבַּע מְאָה
1,000	אֲלַף
10,000	רִבּוֹ
1,000,000	(D 7:10, par. 42) אֲלֶף אַלְפִים
100,000,000	(par. 62) רִבּוֹ רִבְבָן

"Sixty-two" (fem.) is שִׁתִּין וְתַרְתֵּין, "120" מְאָה וְעֶשְׂרִין.

64. "One" follows the noun as an adjective. It may be used to indicate indetermination (par. 46). It may also be used as a noun: חַד מִנְּהוֹן "one of them" D 6:3. Note also כַּחֲדָה "together, without distinction" D 2:35.

65. "Two" has a cstr. st. תְּרֵי, *תַּרְתֵּי.

66. The numerals from three to ten use masc. formations (תְּלָת, etc.) with fem. nouns, and fem. formations (תְּלָתָה, etc.) with masc. nouns.

The cstr. st. is rarely used: שִׁבְעַת יָעֲטֹ֫הִי "his seven advisers" E 7:14, but, for instance, שִׁבְעָה עִדָּנִין "seven seasons" D 4:13.

67. The numerals may either precede or follow the object counted. The latter is in the plural.

68. The det. st. of אֲלַף is אַלְפָּא.

69. The ordinal numbers (with the exception of "second") are adjectives with the ending -āy (par. 58):

	masc.		fem.	
1st	קַדְמִי* (קַדְמָיָא)		קַדְמָיָה* (קַדְמָיְתָא)	
2nd	תִּנְיָן*		תִּנְיָנָה	
3rd	תְּלִיתִי*		תְּלִיתָיָה (t°lītāʾā)	
4th	רְבִיעִי* (רְבִיעָיָא), etc.		רְבִיעָיָה (רְבִיעָיְתָא), etc.	

70. Multiplication is expressed as follows: חַד שִׁבְעָה "seven times" D 3:19.

71. Fractions are represented by the nouns פְּלַג "one-half" D 7:25 and תְּלִתָא "one-third (ruler), triumvir" D 5:16, 29, with suffix תַּלְתִּי D 5:7. The vocalization of תְּלִתָא may, however, have been influenced by Akkadian *šalšu* and may not represent a genuine Aramaic form.

72. "Second" with the adverbial ending *-ūṯ* (par. 88) means "again" (תִּנְיָנוּת D 2:7).

73. תְּלָתֵּהוֹן "the three of them" D 3:23, apparently *t°lāṯ-t*, a fem. form, augmented by the ending of the pl. masc., as happens in connection with some prepositions (par. 84).

74. Dates: The year of the reign and the day of the month are expressed by cardinal numbers following the cstr. st. שְׁנַת and יוֹם, respectively: שְׁנַת שֵׁת לְמַלְכוּת "year 6 of the reign of . . ." E 6:15, יוֹם תְּלָתָה לִירַח אֲדָר "Aḏār 3rd" E 6:15.

The age of a person is expressed by the phrase "son of n years": כְּבַר שְׁנִין שִׁתִּין וְתַרְתֵּין "as (a man) sixty-two years old" D 6:1.

VII. Prepositions

75. BA has the primitive prepositions עִם, עַל, עַד, מִן, לְ, כְּ, בְּ, and others whose derivation from nominal or verbal roots is still obvious.

One-consonant prepositions are written together with the word governed by them. This includes מִן wherever *n* is assimilated to the following consonant.

If the first syllable of the word depending on בכל has a murmured vowel, we have -בְּ, -כְּ, -לְ. Followed by יְ, בכל become -לִי, -בִּי, -כִּי, -לִי.

If the first syllable of the word following בכל has an ultra-short vowel, the corresponding full vowel appears after the preposition: בַּעֲשַׂב "with the vegetation," בֶּאֱסוּר "with a fetter," etc. In connection with אֱלָהּ "god," it is לֶאֱלָהּ שְׁמַיָּא (יִשְׂרָאֵל) E 5:12, 6:9, 10, 7:15, D 2:19, but usually we find בֵּאלָהֵהּ, לֵאלָהָא, etc.; cf. also בֵּאדַֽיִן "then."

76. Certain basic meanings can be established for the prepositions, but, as is only natural, there are no exact correspondences between a given BA preposition and any one English preposition.

In certain constructions, different prepositions may be used with no clearly definable or necessary distinction in meaning. Instances are the alternation between לְ and עַל to indicate the addressee of a letter or document. Further: לְבַקָּרָה עַל יְהוּד וְלִירוּשְׁלֶם "to investigate Judah and Jerusalem" E 7:14, לְדָנִיֵּאל ... אֱלוֹהִי D 6:5f., עַל עַל (קְדָם) "to enter into the presence of" in connection with persons, but עַל לְ in connection with localities (D 6:11). Cf. also מְטָה עַד "he came to" D 7:13 in connection with a person, whereas לְ is commonly used with this verb to indicate direction.

שְׁלֵט "to rule over" is usually followed by בְּ, but עַל occurs in D 2:48. *עֲרַב "to mix with" requires בְּ (D 2:41, 43), but עִם is found in D 2:43. עֲדָה "to come forth" is followed by מִן (D 4:28, 5:20) but also by בְּ (D 3:27), if the text is correct. בְּ and מִן also alternate to express the idea of "being wet with the dew (מְטַל, בְּטַל)" of heaven" D 4:12, 20, 22, 30, 5:21.

77. בְּ "in" (local and temporal), "through, with" (instrumental). With suffixes: בְּהוֹן, בַּהּ, בַּהּ, בָּךְ, בִּי.

Note בְּ אִשְׁתִּי "to drink from (a vessel)" D 5:2, 3, 23, and לָא תִשְׁנֵא צְבוּ בְּדָנִיֵּאל "nothing be changed concerning Daniel" D 6:18.

78. כְּ "like as, comparable to." Also, "according to," as, for instance, repeatedly in כִּדְנָה "thus," כְּדָת מָדַי "according to the law of Media" D 6:9, 13, כִּכְתָב סְפַר מֹשֶׁה "in accordance with the text of the book of Moses" E 6:18. Further, "approximately": כְּשָׁעָה חֲדָה "about an hour (while)" D 4:16.

כְּ may also be used in a temporal sense: כְּבַר שְׁנִין שִׁתִּין וְתַרְתֵּין "as (a man) sixty-two years old" D 6:1, כְּמִקְרְבֵהּ לְגֻבָּא "on approaching the den" D 6:21. Cf. כְּדִי (par. 86).

79. לְ "to, for." With suffixes: לְכֹם (לְכוֹן), לָנָא, לַהּ, לֵהּ, לָךְ, לִי, לְהֹם (לְהוֹן).

לְ expresses every aspect of direction. (a) local: for the addressee of a letter, לְאַרְתַּחְשַׁשְׁתָּא "to Artaxerxes," לְבַיְתֵהּ אֲזַל "he went to his house" D 2:17. (b) temporal: לְעָלְמִין חֱיִי "live for ever." (c) modal: הֲוָת לְטוּר "became a mountain" D 2:35, בְּנַיְתַהּ לְבֵית מַלְכוּ "I have built it for a royal capital" D 4:27. (d) final: אָמְרִין לְעָלָוָן "lambs for sacrifices" E 6:9, מְצַלַּיִן לְחַיֵּי מַלְכָּא "praying for the life of the king" E 6:10.

לְ is commonly used to indicate ownership. It is further used to denote the indirect object and, frequently, the direct object (par. 182). לְ in final meaning usually precedes the infinitive.

80. מִן "from." The *n* is sometimes assimilated to the following consonant. With suffixes: מִנְּהֶן, מִנְּהוֹן, מִנַּהּ, מִנֵּה, מִנָּךְ, מִנִּי.

מִן indicates local direction away from someone or something. It rarely occurs to express temporal direction (מִן יוֹמָת עָלְמָא "since the days of eternity" E 4:15, 19), or causal relationship (מִן טַעַם אֱלָהּ יִשְׂרָאֵל "by the decree of the God of Israel" E 6:14, 7:23).

In the frequent phrase: מִנִּי שִׂים טְעֵם "an order has been given by me," מִן expresses local direction ("an order . . . coming from me"), cf. the variant נִפְקְתָא מִן בֵּית מַלְכָּא תִּתְיְהִב D 6:27, or מִן קֳדָמַי שִׂים טְעֵם "the expenses will be granted by the royal treasury" E 6:4. However, this usage of מִן comes very close to indicating the agent of the passive.

Partitive use of מִן is common: חַד מִנְּהוֹן "one of them" D 6:3, מִן בְּנֵי גָלוּתָא "belonging to the exiles" D 6:14, מִן נִצְבְּתָא "some of the seed (mineral)" D 2:41, מִן קְשֹׁט "it is of a truth" D 2:47, מִן קְצָת ... מִנַּהּ "partly ... partly" D 2:42. In this sense, מִן also corresponds to "than" after a comparative: בְּחָכְמָה דִּי אִיתַי בִּי מִן כָּל חַיַּיָּא "through wisdom that I have (more) than any living being" D 2:30, חֶזְוֵהּ רַב מִן חַבְרָתַהּ "its appearance was great(er) than (that of) its fellows" D 7:20. Cf. also אֲרַע(א) מִנָּךְ "low(er) than you(rs)" D 2:39, עֵלָּא מִנְּהוֹן "high(er) than (above) them" D 6:3.

81. עַד "until" (temporal).
It occurs rarely to indicate local direction: עַד עַתִּיק יוֹמַיָּא מְטָה "to the ancient of days he came" D 7:13, עַד כֹּה "so far" D 7:28. Modal usage appears in עַד כְּסַף כַּכְּרִין מְאָה "up to one hundred talents of silver" E 7:22. Inclusive finality is intended in עַד יוֹמִין תְּלָתִין "for thirty days" D 6:8, 13.

Note the use of וְ "and" in מִן ... וְעַד "from ... to" E 5:16, D 2:20.

82. עַל "upon." With suffixes: עֲלַי, עֲלָיךְ, עֲלוֹהִי, עֲלַיהּ, עֲלַיְנָא, עֲלֵיהֹם (עֲלֵיהוֹן).

In addition to physical location, עַל may indicate mental or modal application: עַל דְּנָה "concerning this" E 4:14, "on account of this" E 4:16, 22, 6:11, עַל רָזָה דְנָה "concerning this secret"

D 2:18, עַל דָּנִיֵּאל שָׂם בָּל "he set his mind on Daniel" D 6:15,
בְּאֵשׁ עֲלוֹהִי "it grieved him" D 6:15, טְאֵב עֲלוֹהִי "it pleased him"
D 6:24.

עַל may indicate direction like לְ (par. 76): מַנְדְּעִי עֲלַי יְתוּב "my
knowledge returned to me" D 4:31, שְׁלַח עַל "to send (a message)
to" E 4:11, 5:17. It may involve hostile direction ("against") or
indicate superior position and greater intensity: חַד שִׁבְעָה עַל
"(heated) seven times more than..." D 3:19, מִתְנַצַּח עַל סָרְכַיָּא
"distinguishing himself over the chief ministers" D 6:4, עַל מַלְכִין
מִתְנַשְּׂאָה "(a city) rising up against (raising itself over) kings"
E 4:19.

83. עִם "together with." With suffixes: עִמִּי, עִמָּךְ, עִמֵּהּ, עִמְּהוֹן.
Temporal use of עִם appears in עִם דָּר וְדָר "in every genera-
tion" D 3:33, 4:31, בְּחֶזְוֵי עִם לֵילְיָא "in my vision in the night"
D 7:2.

Cf., further, עִם מַלְכָּא מַלִּל "he spoke to the king" D 6:22,
עָבְדָה קְרָב עִם קַדִּישִׁין "making war against the holy ones" D 7:21,
לִבְבֵהּ עִם חֵיוְתָא שַׁוִּי (read שַׁוִּיו?) "his heart (mind) was placed with
(= made like) that of an animal" D 5:21, דִּי עֲבַד עִמִּי אֱלָהָא
"(wonders that) God did in connection with me" D 3:32, תַּעַבְדוּן
עִם שָׂבֵי יְהוּדָיֵא "you shall do in dealing with the elders of the Jews"
E 6:8.

84. Other prepositions:

אַחֲרֵי "after" (temporal). With suffix: אַחֲרֵיהוֹן.

בָּתַר, בָּאתַר "after" (temporal), < בְּ+אֲתַר, lit. "in the track(s) of."
With suffix: בָּתְרָךְ.

בֵּין "between." With suffix: בֵּינֵיהֶן. The forms with pronominal
suffixes of בֵּין and some of the following prepositions correspond to
those of the *plural* of the masc. noun; they are formed in analogy
to עַל.

גּוֹא "within," used in composition with בְּ, לְ, and מִן. With
suffixes: בְּגַוֵּהּ, בְּגַוֵּהּ.

דִּי לָא "without," also used before infinitives introduced by לְ
or a prepositional expression.

יַד "hand," in connection with other prepositions, tends to lose
its concrete meaning and assume the character of a preposition.
בְּיַד indicates possession, cf., in particular, דִּי נִשְׁמְתָךְ בִּידֵהּ וְכָל
אָרְחָתָךְ לֵהּ "(God) who holds in His hand your soul and owns all

your ways" D 5:23. Cf. also כְּחָכְמַת אֱלָהָךְ דִּי בִידָךְ "according to the wisdom of your God that is in your hand" E 7:25, יְהַב הִמּוֹ בְּיַד נְבוּכַדְנֶצַּר "He gave them into the hand of Nebuchadnezzar" E 5:12, שֵׁיזִיב ··· מִן יַד אַרְיָוָתָא "he saved ... from the lions" D 6:28.

יָת indicating the independent objective pronoun occurs only once: יָתְהוֹן D 3:12.

לְוָת "with, at (French *chez*)," related to יָת. With suffix: מִן לְוָתָךְ E 4:12.

נֶגֶד "toward" occurs only in נֶגֶד יְרוּשְׁלֶם "toward Jerusalem" D 6:11; possibly a Hebrew gloss.

צַד "side" in combination with לְ and מִן: מִלִּין לְצַד עִלָּיָא יְמַלִּל "he speaks words toward the Most High" D 7:25, מִצַּד מַלְכוּתָא "(to find cause of complaint against Daniel) from the side of the kingdom (= from the political angle)" D 6:5.

לָקֳבֵל "facing, opposite," also in modal use, "corresponding to." With suffix לָקֳבְלָךְ. In the modal sense, it may be augmented by כֹּל: כָּל קֳבֵל דִּי.

קֳדָם "before" (local), also with מִן, "from before." With suffixes (par. 10): וּקְדָמֽוֹהִי; קֳדָמַי (קָדָמַי) קֳדָמָיךְ (qòdāmák), קֳדָמ֫וֹהִי קֳדָמֽוֹהִי (קֳדָמַיהוֹן D 7:13), קֳדָמֵיהוֹן, קֳדָמַיה. קֳדָם is used frequently as a less direct, respectful indication of location (מִן קֳדָם אֱלָהּ שְׁמַיָּא, קֳדָם מַלְכָּא). A possible temporal use occurs in D 7:7.

מִקַּדְמַת, מִן קַדְמַת "before" (temporal).

לִקְצָת "at the end of."

*תַּחַת, תְּחוֹת "underneath." With suffixes: תְּחֹתֵיהִ, תְּחֹתֽוֹהִי.

VIII. Conjunctions

85. Coordinating conjunctions:

וְ "and," connecting words and sentences, is written together with the word that follows it. If the following word begins with a labial (במפ) or has a murmured vowel in the first syllable, וְ becomes וּ (ū). Followed by יְ, *wⁱyⁱ*- becomes וִי-. Followed by a syllable containing an ultra-short vowel, the corresponding full vowel appears after וּ: וַהֲלָךְ "and (a kind of) taxes," וֶאֱתוֹ "and come!," etc. However, it is וֶאֱלָהָא E 6:12 (par. 75), וּסֲגַר "and he locked" D 6:23, וּקְדָמֽוֹהִי D 7:13.

In Babylonian vocalization, w^{e}- remains apparently unchanged before labials and becomes wi- before a word with a murmured vowel in the first syllable.

Strings of coordinated nouns or verbs may be without a co-ordinating particle, or וְ may be used before one, or several, or all components.

בְּרַם, לָהֵן "but." לָהֵן may also be used in the related sense of "except": דִּי לָא יִפְלְחוּן ··· לְכָל אֱלָהּ לָהֵן לֵאלָהֲהוֹן "that they might not worship any God but their own God" D 3:28, ··· מִן כָּל אֱלָהּ וֶאֱנָשׁ לָהֵן מִנָּךְ "from any God or man ... except you" D 6:8, 13.

בֵּאדַיִן, אֱדַיִן "then."

86. Subordinating conjunctions:

דִּי "that" introduces subordinate clauses after verbs meaning to know, inform, command, find, see, hear, etc. Cf. also אִיתַי דִּי "it is (a fact) that" E 5:17, מִן קְשֹׁט דִּי "it is of a truth that" D 2:47, אָזְדָּא מִנִּי מִלְּתָא דִּי "the matter is known (as decided), as far as I am concerned, that" D 2:8f. (cf. D 2:5, where the Dead Sea [Qumrān] text inserts דִי after אזדא).

דִּי is further used to introduce final clauses ("so that" E 5:10, 6:10, D 2:18, 3:28, 6:18). It is causal in D 2:47, 4:15, 6:24. It may also introduce direct speech (D 2:25, 5:7, 6:6, 8, 14). Note בְּעִדָּנָא דִּי "at the time when" D 3:5, 15.

כְּדִי "when" (temporal, but tending occasionally toward a causal meaning).

מִן דִּי "after, as soon as," occasionally causal as in D 3:22.

כָּל קֳבֵל דִּי "because," but in D 5:22 "although."

הֵא כְדִי "as" D 2:43, spelled as if it were *ha-$k^{e}di$, but to be pronounced as derived from $h\bar{e}k$-di.

עַד דִּי "until," also simple עַד E 4:21, 5:5, tending toward a final connotation in D 4:22.

עַל דִּבְרַת דִּי (D 2:30), עַד דִּבְרַת דִּי (D 4:14) (= $^{c}addi\underline{b}ra\underline{t} < ^{c}al$-$di\underline{b}ra\underline{t}$) "so that."

דִּי לְמָה (E 4:22), דִּי לְמָה (E 7:23) "lest."

הֵן "if." In D 3:15 (הֵן ··· הֵן לָא "if ... if not"), the apodosis for the positive alternative is left unstated (supply "it is well and good"). הֵן ··· הֵן may mean "either ... or": הֵן לְמוֹת הֵן לִשְׁרֹשִׁי הֵן לַעֲנָשׁ נִכְסִין וְלֶאֱסוּרִין "(will be sentenced) either to death or to corporal punishment or to a property fine and imprisonment" E 7:26.

IX. Negations

87. לָא is used in connection with negative statements. It may also be used for the negation of individual parts of a sentence.

It is used as a noun in אַרְעָא כְּלָה חֲשִׁיבִין (*dāyᵉrē*) כָּל דָּאֲרֵי "all inhabitants of the earth are considered like nought" D 4:32.

אַל is used with the jussive to express a negative wish or command. The imperative cannot be employed with negation. אַל was discarded in later Aramaic and replaced by לָא. A possible but doubtful example of this process in E 4:21: קִרְיְתָא דָךְ לָא תִתְבְּנֵא "let that city not be rebuilt."

For לְמָה "lest," cf. par. 86, and for דִּי לָא "without" (also simple לָא before an infinitive, D 6:16), cf. par. 84.

X. Adverbs and Particles

88. Adverbs may be expressed by prepositional expressions or by special words. In addition, they may be formed by

(1) an ancient fem. formation showing retention of final -*t*: טְוָת "(he spent the night) fasting" D 6:19.

(2) the ending -*ūṯ*: תִּנְיָנוּת "a second time, again" D 2:7.

(3) the abs. st. masc., as in the frequent שַׂגִּיא "much, greatly, very": קְצַף שַׂגִּיא "he became very angry" D 2:12, שַׂגִּיא מִתְבְּהַל "greatly disturbed" D 5:9 (par. 20), etc. A further example may be גְּמִיר "completely" (= and so on, with all the proper formulas of greeting to be supplied) E 7:12.

(4) the ending -*ā*, mostly unstressed, the remnant of an ancient accusative ending: אֵזֵא יַתִּירָא "heated excessively" D 3:22, תַּקִּיפָא (*yattīrā*!) יַתִּירָא "exceedingly strong" (fem.) D 7:7, דְּחִילָה יַתִּירָה "very frightening" (fem.) D 7:19. Further, אַרְעָא (*árᵉā*, read *ᵉraᵉ*) "below" and עֵלָּא "above" (par. 80), and, possibly, יַצִּיבָא in D 3:24, מַלְכָּא (*yaṣṣībā*!) יַצִּיבָא "certainly, O king" (cf. מִן יַצִּיב יָדַע אֲנָה "I know for certain" D 2:8). For כֹּלָּא, see par. 96. The final -*ā* of some Persian loan words was apparently considered the same ending (par. 189).

89. Temporal demonstrative adverbs:

בֵּאדַ֫יִן, אֱדַ֫יִן "then," used by itself as a coordinating conjunction (par. 85), but וֶאֱדַ֫יִן "and then" E 5:5.

כְּעֶ֫נֶת, כְּעַן (E 4:10, 11, 7:12), כְּעֶת (E 4:17) "now, now then."

עַד אַחֲרֵין "eventually" D 4:5.

בַּהּ שַׁעֲתָא, בַּהּ זִמְנָא "at once," lit. "at this very hour (time, moment)." ה here represents the demonstrative element hā and was assimilated to the pronominal suffixes (par. 32), used in the proleptic manner found, for instance, in בַּהּ בְּלֵילְיָא "in this very night" D 5:30 and בַּהּ בְּדָנִיֵּאל "in Daniel" D 5:12. The demonstrative construction is still reflected in מִנַּהּ מַלְכוּתָה "from (this) kingdom" D 7:24.

90. Temporal assertive adverb:

עוֹד "still, yet": עוֹד מִלְּתָא בְּפֻם מַלְכָּא "the word still (being) in the mouth of the king" D 4:28.

91. Local demonstrative adverbs:

הָא "behold here": הָא אֲנָה חָזֵה "behold, I see" D 3:25.

אֲרוּ, אֲלוּ "behold there (is)."

כֹּה "here" D 7:28.

תַּמָּה "there," מִן תַּמָּה "from there."

אֲתַר דִּי "there where," lit., "on the spot where" E 6:3, a use possibly influenced by Akkadian ašar "where."

92. Modal demonstrative adverbs:

כְּנֵ֫מָא, כֵּן, כִּדְנָה "thus."

כְּמָה "how!": אָתֹ֫והִי כְּמָה רַבְרְבִין וְתִמְהֹ֫והִי כְּמָה תַקִּיפִין "how great are His wonders, and how mighty are His miracles!" D 3:33.

93. Modal assertive adverbs:

אַף "also."

אַפְּתֹם "certainly" or "finally" E 4:13 (par. 190).

אָסְפַּרְנָא (ʾospárnā) "exactly, perfectly" (par. 189).

אַדְרַזְדָּא "diligently" (par. 189).

הַצְדָּא D 3:14 is often explained as the interrogative particle with an adverb *צדא, possibly meaning "truly" (?).

כַּחֲדָה "together, without distinction" (par. 64).

אָזְדָּא "publicly known, known (as decided)" (par. 189) is originally an adverb.

94. The interrogative particle is -הֲ, with the negation הֲלָא. -הַ for -הֲ is found before words with a murmured vowel in the first syllable and before words beginning with א. Presumably, -הַ would also appear before words beginning with a laryngal.

XI. אִיתַי

95. אִיתַי indicates existence ("there is, exists"), or, with negation (לָא אִיתַי) "there does not exist"). In this meaning, אִיתַי remains unchanged. Cf. אִיתַי גֻּבְרִין יְהוּדָאִין "there are Jewish men" D 3:12, חׇכְמָה דִּי אִיתַי בִּי "wisdom that exists in me" D 2:30; further, הֵן אִיתַי דִּי "whether it is (a fact) that" E 5:17.

However, אִיתַי may take the place of the copula (which, as a rule, is left unexpressed in BA, or is expressed by the independent personal pronoun [par. 30]). In this case, it takes the appropriate pronominal suffix. Originally, אִיתַי here was used for emphasis: הַאִיתָיךְ כָּהֵל "*are* you able?" D 2:26, מְדׇרְהוֹן עִם בִּשְׂרָא לָא אִיתוֹהִי "their dwelling is *not* with human kind" D 2:11, לָא אִיתֶינָא פׇלְחִין "we shall *not* worship" D 3:18, לָא אִיתֵיכוֹן פׇלְחִין "you do *not* worship" D 3:14, אִיתֵיכוֹן עֲתִידִין "you *are* ready" D 3:15.

XII. כֹּל and אׇחֳרָן

96. כֹּל (unstressed כָּל) is a noun meaning "totality." Cf. כֹּלָּא (*kọ́llā*) "everything, everyone" D 2:40, 4:9, 18, 25. This form may also be used in a quasi-adverbial manner: שְׁלָמָא כֹלָּא "well-being completely" E 5:7.

Preceding a sg. noun without the article, it means "every, any." Preceding a determined noun in the sg., it means "entire, whole." And preceding a determined noun in the pl. or a collective sg. (i.e., כָּל בִּשְׂרָא "all mankind"), or being followed by the pl. of the pronominal suffix, or the relative pronoun, or the demon-

4 *

strative pronoun used as a noun (כָּל דְּנָה "all this"), it means "all."

Note that כָּל קֳבֵל has nothing to do with כֹּל (par. 84).

97. אָחֳרָן "other" may be used either as a noun or as an adjective. Its fem. is אָחֳרִי (par. 57).

XIII. The Verb

98. The BA verb possesses two tenses: a "perfect" to indicate completed action, corresponding to the English present perfect, simple past, and past perfect, and an "imperfect" to indicate incomplete ("im-perfect") action, corresponding to our present or future. It further has a participle, which moreover serves widely as a multi-purpose tense (par. 177). It has two moods, an imperative and a jussive; and an infinitive. There are two voices, active and passive.

99. In addition to its basic form, the BA verb has two "derived conjugations," that is, modifications of the basic root to express modes of action. This is achieved by doubling of the second consonant of the root, or by the addition of a prefix. Each conjugation, furthermore, can form a reflexive/passive by prefixing the element *t-* (*hiṯ-*, *'iṯ-*). Thus, the conjugations are:

pᵊ'al	hiṯpᵊ'el	Passive: pᵊ'īl
pa''el	hiṯpa''al	*pu''al
hap̄'el	*hiṯhap̄'al	hu/op̄'al

The basic meaning of the pa''el is intensive or causative, and that of the hap̄'el, causative.

Beginning *h* alternates with the glottal stop, but forms with *h* are more widely used in the BA text.

Since the reflexive of the hap̄'el is not attested in BA (except by doubtful textual correction of E 4:13, מַלְכִים תְּהַנְזִק to מַלְכִי מַתהנזק), its form is somewhat uncertain.

For remnants of the šap̄'el (corresponding in meaning to the hap̄'el) and hištap̄'al, cf. par. 157 and 166.

100. The verbal conjugation follows an identical scheme for all roots. Minor irregularities occur principally in connection with roots that contain a glottal stop; that have *n* as the first consonant; and which consisted originally of two consonants made triconsonantal by the addition of *w/y* or by doubling of the second consonant. These are the "weak" verbs, as opposed to the regular "strong" verb.

1. The strong verb

Cf. the paradigms, pp. 60—63.

101. The perfect is formed with the help of suffixed elements:

sg. 3. masc.			כְּתַב
3. fem.	-*at*		כֶּתְבַת
2. masc.	-*t* (-*tā*)		כְּתַבְתְּ (כְּתַבְתָּ, -תָּה)
2. fem.	-*tī*		כְּתַבְתִּי*
1.	-*ēt*		כִּתְבֵת
pl. 3. masc.	-*ū*		כְּתַבוּ
3. fem.	-*ā* (par. 12)		כְּתַבָה
2. masc.	-*tūn*		כְּתַבְתּוּן
2. fem.	-*tēn*		כְּתַבְתֵּן
1.	-*nā*		כְּתַבְנָא

102. In addition to the pᵉ‘al with *a* in the second syllable, there also exists a pᵉ‘e/il: סְגִד "prostrated himself," שְׁלִם "was completed," שְׁלֵט "had power," pl. שְׁלִטוּ. For the 3. fem. sg., besides תְּקְפַת (from תְּקֵף "was strong"), we find בְּטֵלַת "was idle." The vocalization בְּטֵלַת corresponds to what in later Jewish Aramaic is the normal vocalization of the 3. fem. sg. (*pᵉ‘a/ēlat*).

For the passive forms and the derived conjugations, cf. the paradigms.

103. *ē* and *i* may apparently be used interchangeably in the pᵉ‘el, hitpᵉ‘el, pa‘‘el, and hap̄‘el.

104. The 3. fem. sg. of the derived conjugations is attested only with verbs ending in laryngals or *r* and other weak verbs

(הַדֶּקֶת, הִתְגּוֹרַת, etc.). These forms do not seem normative (at least, not for the period of Official Aramaic), and the normal form presumably was *הִתְכַּתְּבַת, etc.

105. The imperfect (jussive, par. 108) uses prefixes, supplemented in some of its forms by suffixes:

sg. 3. masc.	*y-*		יִכְתֻּב
3. fem.	*t-*		תִּכְתֻּב
2. masc.	*t-*		תִּכְתֻּב
2. fem.	*t---īn*		*תִּכְתֻּבִין
1.	*ˀ-*		אֶכְתֻּב
pl. 3. masc.	*y---ūn*		יִכְתְּבוּן
3. fem.	*y---ān*		יִכְתְּבָן
2. masc.	*t---ūn*		תִּכְתְּבוּן
2. fem.	*t---ān*		*תִּכְתְּבָן
1.	*n-*		נִכְתֻּב

For the use of the prefix *l-*, instead of *y-*, see par. 168.

106. No practical rules can be formulated for the vowel following the second consonant of the root. Most verbs p^{ec}al have *u*. P^{ec}el verbs prefer *a*, but cf., for instance, יִסְגֻּד – סְגֵד. For imperfects with *ẹ*, cf. par. 118.

107. No passive forms of the imperfect happen to occur in BA.

108. The jussive is indicated only in a few forms by the elision of final *-n* in the 3. masc. pl. Only weak verbs happen to be attested: יֵאבַדוּ "let them perish" Jer. 10:11, אַל יִשְׁתַּנּוֹ "let them not be changed" D 5:10, with pronominal suffix אַל יְבַהֲלוּךְ "let them not disturb you" D 5:10. The form of the suffix in אַל יְבַהֲלָךְ "let it not disturb you" D 4:16 indicates the jussive, as the indicative would be *יְבַהֲלִנָּךְ (par. 175). Finally, the spelling with final *-y* in יִתְקְרֵי "let him be called" D 5:12 may be the remnant of an old jussive form (par. 152).

109. In the hitp^{ec}el and hitpa^{cc}al, the imperfect prefix + *(h)it-* becomes *yit-*, etc. In the hap̄^cel, *h* is retained, but the ˀap̄^cel has the imperfect *ya-*, etc.

110. The imperative has the same vowel after the second consonant of the root as is found in the imperfect (jussive), and endings corresponding to those of the jussive:

sg. 2. masc.		כְּתֻב, שְׁלֻט
2. fem.	-ī	כְּתֻ֫בִי
pl. 2. masc.	-ū	כְּתֻ֫בוּ
2. fem.	-ā	כְּתֻ֫בָה*

The imperative cannot be used in connection with a negation. In order to express a negated imperative, the jussive (imperfect) must be used (par. 87).

111. The infinitive of the pᵉ῾al has the preformative *m*- (מִכְתַּב). A remnant of an older form without *m*- is לִבְנֵא (par. 149).

In the derived conjugations, a fem. formation serves as infinitive (*p...῾ālā*). The cstr. st. ending -*aṯ* is preserved only in לְהַנְזָקַת מַלְכִין "to cause harm to kings" E 4:22 and אַחֲוָיַת אֲחִידָן "giving information on riddles" D 5:12. Elsewhere, it is replaced by -*ūṯ*, for instance, הִתְנַדָּבוּת "contributing" E 7:16, לְהוֹדָעוּתָךְ "to let you know" E 5:10.

Forms such as מַצְלַח "to succeed" E 5:8 and מְפַשַּׁר "to interpret," מְשָׁרֵא "to solve" D 5:12, may be further infinitive formations of the derived conjugations, but this is uncertain, as is the assumption that אֶשְׁתַּדּוּר "rebellion" E 4:15 is an infinitive of the hitpa῾῾al of the root שדר (cf. par. 190 for a Persian etymology).

112. The participles may be used and declined as any noun or adjective.

113. For the addition of pronominal suffixes, cf. par. 174ff. and the paradigms, p. 71.

2. Roots beginning with a sibilant or dental

114. The reflexive *t* is placed after the sibilant: מִשְׁתַּבְּשִׁין "confused," תִּשְׁתְּבִק "will be left," הִשְׁתְּכַח "was found," מִשְׁתַּכַּל "observing."

It assimilates to the emphatic pronunciation of צ and becomes ט: יִצְטַבַּע "will be wetted."

It assimilates fully to ז in הַזְמִנְתּוּן "you have agreed upon" D 2:9. The written form represents *hizzᵉmintūn* or *hizzammintūn*, while the reading prescribed assumes only partial assimilation of *t > d, hizdᵊmintūn*.

The situation is different with roots having *w/y* as the second consonant (par. 138).

Assimilation can also be expected in roots beginning with a dental, but no relevant forms are found in BA.

3. Roots containing a laryngal or ר

115. In connection with these roots, note the rules mentioned in par. 24 (preceding *e/i > a*) and par. 20 (lengthening of preceding vowel instead of gemination): פְּלַח "worshiping," מְשַׁבַּח "praising" (identical in form with the passive participle), אֲמַר "saying," בְּרִךְ (< *barrik*) "he blessed," etc.

In roots ending in a laryngal or ר, the change *e/i > a* is extended to open syllables: שַׁבַּחוּ "they praised," הַשְׁכַּחוּ "they found," אַתָּרוּ "shake off!" (pl.), בַּדַּרוּ "scatter!" (pl.), אֶתְעֲקַרָה "they (fem.) were uprooted."

116. In addition, the following differences affecting the vocalization may be noted:

Roots with a laryngal as the first consonant have *a* in the perfect pᵉ'al, 1. sg. (and 3. fem. sg.): עֲבְדֵת "I have made."

The prefix vowel of the imperfect is *a* (e in verbs with י/*w/y* as the third consonant of the root): תַּעַבְדוּן "you will do," תֶּעְדֵּא "it (fem.) will pass away."

The prefix vowel of the infinitive is *e*: לְמֶעְבַּד "to do," לְמֶחֱזֵא "to behold."

Where the laryngal is originally vowelless after a prefix and the following consonant has a murmured vowel, the laryngal may take the vowel of the prefix: תַּעַבְדוּן (< *taᶜbᵊdūn*), הָחָרְבַת (*hohorbaṯ* < *hohrᵊbaṯ*) "was destroyed". But cf. יַחְסְנוּן "they will possess," מְהַחְצְפָה "urgent" (fem.).

e for *a* occurs in הֶחֱסְנוּ "they took possession" D 7:22, הֶעְדִּיו "they removed" D 5:20, 7:12.

117. Roots ending in a laryngal or ר tend to eliminate a final cluster of consonants, such as is usual in the 2. masc. sg. of the perfect, by the insertion of an anaptyctic vowel: הִשְׁתְּכַחַתְּ "you were found" D 5:27 (but, with retention of the final vowel, שַׁבַּחְתְּ "you praised" D 5:23). Cf. the similar phenomenon in the noun (par. 51).

This vocalization has been transferred to the 3. fem. sg. and 1. sg.: אַמְרֶת "she said" D 5:10, (-אָת) הִתְגְּזֶרֶת "it (fem.) broke off" D 2:34, 45, הִשְׁתְּכַחַת "it (fem.) was found" D 5:11, etc., הַשְׁכַּחַת "I have found" D 2:25. However, we also find יִדְעֵת "I knew," שַׁבְּחֵת "I praised." Cf. also הַדֵּקֶת, הֲקֵמֶת, שָׂמֶת (par. 133, 140, 164).

4. Roots beginning with נ

118. In connection with these roots, cf. par. 21 (assimilation/ nasalization of vowelless *n*): יִנְתְּנוּן "they will give" E 4:13, but also יִתְּנִנּה "he gives it" D 4:14, 22, 29.

ẹ as the vowel of the imperfect pᵃʿal is found in נפל "to fall" and נתן "to give": יִפֵּל (unstressed יִפֵּל לָךְ *yippellāḵ* E 7:20), יִנְתֵּן, תִּנְתֵּן. Cf. also שָׂא "take!" (par. 126).

Only the imperfect and the infinitive of the root נתן occur in BA; for the perfect and imperative, another root, יהב, is used (par. 129).

119. The imperative drops the נ: פֻּקוּ "come out!" (pl.) D 3:26, שָׂא "take!" E 5:15.

5. Roots beginning with א

120. The vowel *a* appears in the pᵃʿal perfect, 1. sg.: אַמְרֵת "I said" D 4:5. For the 3. fem. sg., where the same vocalization can be expected (אַמְרַת*), the only example available is again from a root ending in ר: אַמְרֶת "she said" D 5:10 (par. 117).

121. In the imperfect and infinitive of the pᵃʿal, the vowelless glottal stop becomes silent, and the preceding vowel is lengthened: יֵאמַר, נֵאמַר, תֵּאמְרוּן, יֵאבַדוּ "let them perish" Jer. 10:11, מֵאמַר (מֵמַר E 5:11), לְמֵזֵא "to heat" D 3:19.

122. The imperative pᵃʿal with *a* after the second consonant has *ᵉ* in the first syllable, the one with *u* has *ᵃ*: אֱמַר, אֱמָרוּ, but אֲכֻלִי "eat!" (fem.) D 7:5.

Full *ẹ* (with secondary stress) appears in the case of an imperative with *e* after the second consonant: אֱזֵל (*ʾèzel-*) "go!" E 5:15.

123. The part. pass. pᵉ῾al can be expected to have been *אָמִיר,
but *ẹ* appears in the first syllable of the only form attested (of a
root ending in *w/y*): אֲזֵה "heated" D 3:22.

124. In the hap̄῾el, *hō̆-* (< *haw-*) replaces *ha-ʾ: *הוֹבֵד, תְּהוֹבֵד,
לְהוֹבָדָה, יְהוֹבִדוּן "to destroy." The passive is הוּבַד "was destroyed"
D 7:11.

Two roots, אמן and אתה, show *hẹ̄-* and *hay-*: הֵימִן "he believed"
D 6:24, מְהֵימַן "trusted, trustworthy" D 2:45, 6:5, הַיְתִי "he brought,"
passive הֵיתָיִת, הֵיתָיִו (par. 167).

6. Roots with א as the second consonant

125. None of the forms attested shows any irregularity: שְׁאֵל
"he asked," שְׁאֶלְנָא, שְׁאֵל, יִשְׁאֲלֶנְכוֹן "he will ask you," בְּאֵשׁ "was bad,"
טְאֵב "was good."

7. Roots with final א

126. Most of these roots have merged with those originally ending
in *w/y*. Since their forms can no longer be distinguished from those
of the latter, they are treated together with them (par. 144ff.).

Remnants of roots ending in א that have preserved א as a consonant are שֵׂא (נשא) "take!" E 5:15, מִתְנַשְּׂאָה "rising up" [fem.]
E 4:19) and שׂנא "to hate" (שָׂנְאֵיךְ "your enemies" D 4:16).

8. Roots beginning with י

127. In Aramaic (and Canaanite), initial *w* has been replaced
by *y*, so that all roots originally beginning with *w* have merged
with those beginning with *y*.

128. In the imperfect (and infinitive) of the pᵉ῾al, vowelless י is
replaced by gemination/nasalization of the second consonant in the
ancient roots יְדַע "to know" and יְתֵב "to sit": יִנְדְּעוּן, אֶנְדַּע, תִנְדַּע,
יִתֵּב D 7:26; cf. also the noun מַנְדַּע "knowledge." Further יִכֻּל,
from the root יְכֻל "to be able" (par. 171).

Another imperfect formation is attested only through יֵיטַב "it is
good, pleases" E 7:18, from an ancient secondary root יטב (cf.
טָאֵב, טָב).

129. Verbs forming the imperfect with gemination/nasalization of the second consonant drop י in the imperative: דַּע "know!" D 6:16, הַב "give!" D 5:17 (from the root יהב which, for the imperfect and infinitive, is replaced by נתן [par. 118]). Cf. also the nouns עֵטָה "advice," שְׁנָתֵּהּ "his sleep," representing old infinitive formations of יעט, ישׁן.

130. The hap̄ʿel has *hō̆-* (< *haw-*): הוֹדַע "he informed," יְהוֹדַע, הוֹתֵב, לְהוֹדָעָה, מְהוֹדְעִין "he settled (them)," מוֹדֵא, מְהוֹדֵא "praising." The passive is הוּסְפַת "was added" (fem.) D 4:33.

hē̆- is found only in הֵיבֵל "he brought" E 5:14, לְהֵיבָלָה E 7:15. The same root may be present also in מְסוֹבְלִין "(foundations) laid" E 6:3, as a šap̄ʿel borrowed from Akkadian (par. 188).

9. Roots with ו or י as the second consonant

Cf. the paradigms, pp. 64—65.

131. Formations of roots with *y* as the second consonant have, in many instances, become identical with those of roots containing *w*. Therefore, it is convenient to treat the two groups of verbs together.

132. In some roots, ו functions as a consonant: תְּוַהּ "he was perturbed" and, in roots with final *y*, הֲוָה "he was," *חֲוִי "he informed," שַׁוִּי, יִשְׁתַּוֵּה "to place, make."

133. Long *ā* is found throughout the perfect pᵉʿal: קָם "he rose" (root *qwm*), שָׂם "he placed" (root *śym*), בָּת "he spent the night" (root *byt*). A pᵉʿe/il is רָם "(his heart) was haughty" (root *rwm*) D 5:20.

The 1. sg. is שָׂמֵת (< *śāmt*) E 6:12.

There is a passive form שֻׂמַת "it (fem.) was placed" D 6:18. This makes it doubtful whether the frequent שִׂים is a perfect passive, or rather the participle passive.

134. The imperfect pᵉʿal has *ū* throughout (יְקוּם), and, presumably, *ī* in roots containing *y* (*יְשִׂים). An *ā* imperfect occurs in יְהָךְ "he will go" (par. 169).

135. The imperative is *קוּם, קוּמִי, and *שִׂים, שִׂימוּ.

136. The infinitive has the form *מְקָם, *מְשָׂם, cf. מְהָךְ (par. 169).

137. In the active participle of the pᵊꜥal, *w/y* is replaced by the glottal stop (קָאֵם). In the other forms where א has a murmured vowel, א remains in writing, but the reading prescribed by the Masoretes is י: קָאֲמִין (*qāyᵊmin*), דָּאֲנִין (*dāyᵊnin*) "judging," דָּאֲרֵי (*dāyᵊrē*) "dwellers of." But קָאֲמַיָּא D 7:16, where the main word stress does not immediately follow the syllable containing ᵊ/*y*.

138. The hitpᵊꜥel shows gemination of the preformative *t*, and either *i* or *ā* after the first consonant of the root: יִתְּזִין "obtains food" D 4:9, but מִתְּשָׁם, יִתְּשָׁם.

139. The paꜥꜥel of *qwm* is לְקַיָּמָה, קַיֵּם *, with י instead of ו. In all other respects, both paꜥꜥel and hitpaꜥꜥal of these roots are like those of the strong verb.

140. The perfect of the hap̄ꜥel shows vacillation between *i* and *ē* after the first consonant of the root: הֲקִים, אֲקִימֵה "he set (it) up." The 1. sg. is הֲקֵימֵת D 3:14.

The passive is הֻקְמַת (fem.) D 7:5, הֲקִימַת D 7:4. It has been suggested that the first form be read *הֲקִמַת (and be transferred to D 7:4), and the second as the active *הֲקִימַת (and be transferred to D 7:5).

141. The imperfect, the participle, and, presumably, the imperative of the hap̄ꜥel show the same vacillation between *i* and *ē*. In addition, an unusual long *ā* (par. 23) appears after the preformative in some cases: יְתִיבוּן, יַהֲתִיבוּן "they will return, give back" E 5:5, 6:5, יְקִים, יְהָקֵים, מְהָקֵים, תָּסֵיף "it (fem.) will bring to an end," מְרִים "raising up," מְגִיחָן "stirring up" (pl. fem.).

142. The infinitive of the hap̄ꜥel is לְהַזָדָה "to act impiously" D 5:20, לְהָקָמוּתֵהּ "to set him up" D 6:4, לַהֲתָבוּתָךְ "to render (a reply) to you" D 3:16.

143. A remnant of a derived conjugation, formed with reduplication of the last consonant, appears in מְרוֹמֵם "exalting" D 4:34, הִתְרוֹמַ֫מְתָּ "you exalted yourself" D 5:23 (cf. par. 157).

10. Roots ending in ו/ᵊ or א

Cf. the paradigms, pp. 66—68.

144. Roots originally ending in ו/ᵊ and א have merged in BA, with some isolated exceptions for those ending in א (par. 126).

The spelling of final *ā* and *ẹ̄* in forms of these roots vacillates between ה and א.

145. The pᵊ῾al has two formations in the perfect, corresponding to pᵊ῾al and pᵊ῾e/il. The second is represented only by the forms אִשְׁתִּיו "they drank" D 5:3 f. and צְבִית "I wished" D 7:19. The perfect of the pᵊ῾al formation has the endings -*ā*, -*āṯ*, and -*ọ̄* for the 3. masc. sg., 3. fem. sg., and 3. masc. pl., respectively. The diphthong *ay* is retained in the 2. sg., but contracted to *ẹ̄* in the 2. pl. and the 1. sg. and pl.

Note רְבִית "you have grown" D 4:19, where the consonants indicate the usual form רְבֵית, while the reading suggested is רְבַת. הֲוַת "it (fem.) was" D 2:35 is doubtful and, probably, should be הֲוָת.

146. The passive pᵊ῾al is represented by גְּלִי, גֶּלִי, "was revealed," and קְרִי "was read."

147. The imperfect forms without suffixed elements end in -*ẹ̄* (< -*ay*). The 2. and 3. masc. pl. end in -*ọ̄n* (< -*awn* < -*ayūn*), while the corresponding fem. forms retain *y* as a consonant. However, the 2. masc. pl. with pronominal suffix is תְּהַחֲוֻנַּנִי (*tᵊhaḥᵃwunnáni* [par. 175]) "you will let me know" D 2:9, with *u* instead of *ọ̄/ọ*.

For forms with the prefix *l-* in connection with הוה, see par. 168.

148. The imperative pᵊ῾al is represented by חֱיִי "live!," הֱוֹו "be!" (pl.) E 4:22 (הֱוֹו E 6:6), אֱתוֹ "come!" (pl.) D 3:26.

149. The infinitive pᵊ῾al ends in -*ẹ̄* (< -*ay*): לְמִבְנָא "to build." An ancient form without preformative is attested in לִבְנָא E 5:3,13 (originally *bᵊnā*?). A form expanded into the det. st. is לְמִבְנְיָה E 5:9.

Forms with pronominal suffixes restore *y*: כְּמִצְבְּיֵה "as he wishes" D 4:32, לְמֵזְיֵה "to heat it" D 3:19.

150. The active participle is (אָ-) עָנֵה "answering," fem. שָׁנְיָה "being different," pl. masc. שָׁתַן "drinking," fem. שָׁנְיָן "being different."

The passive participle is שְׁרֵא "residing," בְּנֵה "built" (בְּנָיָה, בַּנְיָה, בְּנָיָן).

151. The perfect of the derived conjugations ends in -*ī*, retained throughout.

The 3. fem. sg. is represented only by the (h)itpᵊ῾el אֶתְכְּרִיַת "(my spirit) became sick" D 7:15. Whether this vocalization is exceptional, instead of an expected *הִתְבְּנֵית, or whether it is to be considered the normal form in BA (as it is in later Jewish Aramaic) cannot now be decided (par. 102, 104, 117).

The passive of a derived conjugation is represented by הֵיתָית הֵיתָיִי (par. 167).

152. The formation of the imperfect of the derived conjugations corresponds to that of the pᵊᶜal.

A jussive is attested in אַל יִשְׁתַּנּוֹ "let them not be changed" D 5:10. In יִתְקְרֵי "let him be called" D 5:12, the spelling with י, instead of א/ה, may indicate a jussive, although such orthographic distinction had become obscured already at an early date.

153. The imperative of the derived conjugations is attested by מֶּנִּי (*ménni*) "appoint!" E 7:25 and הַחֲוֹנִי "let me know!" (pl.) D 2:6.

154. The infinitives of the derived conjugations retain י as a consonant.

155. The endings of the active participles of the derived conjugations correspond to those of the pᵊᶜal. The sg. masc. of the passive participles of the paᶜᶜel and the hap̄ᶜel may have been מְהַבְנִי***, מְבַנִּי**.

156. For the addition of pronominal suffixes, see par. 176 and the paradigms, p. 71.

11. Roots with identical second and third consonants

Cf. the paradigms, pp. 69—70.

157. Certain verbs of this type seem to have been treated like the strong verb, cf. the (h)ap̄ᶜel תַּטְלֵל ("the animals) seek shade (shelter)" D 4:9. This applies to the šap̄ᶜel, borrowed from Akkadian, שַׁכְלִלוּ "they completed," שַׁכְלְלֵה "he completed it," לְשַׁכְלָלָה, יִשְׁתַּכְלְלוּן. It also applies to formations such as אֶשְׁתּוֹמֵם "he was perturbed" (root *šmm*) D 4:16 and הִתְרוֹמַּמְתָּ, מְרוֹמֵם (par. 143).

158. The perfect pᵊᶜal shows contraction of the identical consonants in the 3. masc. sg. and pl. Contraction also takes place in other forms where the two identical consonants are separated only by a murmured vowel reduced to zero, but original separatedness

may be indicated in the written form: עַל "he entered," עֲלַלת
(ʿalʾlat, read ʿallat) "she entered" D 5:10, but נַדַּת "(his sleep) fled"
D 6:19. דָּקוּ "they were crushed" D 2:35 (as if derived from a
root dwq) should be דָּקּוּ.

159. The imperfect, and all other forms with preformatives, are
characterized by transference of the gemination from the second/
third to the first consonant of the root: תֵּרֹעַ (< tirroʿ) "(the kingdom) will break" D 2:40. Cf. also the noun מֶעָלֵי (mèʿʿālḗ) "the
entrance (setting) of (the sun)" D 6:15.

160. The imperative shows contraction as in the perfect: גֹּדּוּ
"cut down!" (pl.) D 4:11, 20.

161. The infinitive is attested in מְחַן (miḥḥan) "to show mercy"
D 4:24.

162. The active participle pᵉʿal is formed like that of the strong
verb, but the kᵉtib suggests contraction for forms augmented by
endings: עֲלֲלִין (ʿālʾlin, read ʿallin) "entering" (pl.) D 4:4, 5:8.

163. The hitpᵉʿel is not attested. All forms of the paʿʿel and the
hitpaʿʿal correspond to those of the strong verb.

164. The haphʿel requires gemination/nasalization of the first consonant of the root (par. 159): הַנְעֵל "he brought in" D 2:25, הַעֵלְנִי
"let me enter!" D 2:24, הַדֵּקֶת, הַדֵּקֶת "it (fem.) crushed" D 2:34, 45,
הַדִּקוּ D 6:25, תַּדִּק D 2:40, 44, תַּדְּקַנֵּה "(the kingdom) will crush it
(the earth)" D 7:23, infinitive לְהַנְעָלָה,לְהֶעָלָה, participle מְהַדֵּק,
מַדְּקָה,מַדֵּקָה. For the passive, cf. הֻעַל (huʿʿal) "he was brought in"
D 5:13, הֻעָלוּ (huʿʿālū, possibly הֻעָלוּ, but not הֶעֱלוּ) D 5:15.

12. Some special irregular verbs

165. Many roots combine two of the afore-mentioned irregularities. They have been mentioned under the one or the other,
or both, relevant categories before.

166. Šapʿel formations: In addition to שַׁכְלֵל (par. 157) and
מְסוֹבְלִין (par. 130), BA has two more šapʿel formations borrowed
from Akkadian, שֵׁיצִי(א) "to complete" (root wdʾ) and שֵׁיזִב "to save"
(root ʿzb) (לְשֵׁיזָבוּתֵהּ, מְשֵׁיזִב, יְשֵׁיזְבִנְכוֹן, יְשֵׁיזְבִנֵּהּ, יְשֵׁיזִב).

167. אֲתָה "to come" has the hap̄ʿel הַיְתִי, הַיְתִיוּ, לְהַיְתָיָה, passive הֵיתָיִת (fem.) D 6:18, הֵיתָיוּ D 3:13.

168. הֲוָה "to be" uses forms of the imperfect with a preformative ל instead of the usual יְ: לְהֶוֵא, לֶהֱוֹן, לֶהֱוֵין.

169. *הלך "to go" is represented by participles of the paʿʿel and the hap̄ʿel, מְהַלֵּךְ, מַהְלְכִין (to be corrected to מְהַלְכִין?). The imperfect and infinitive pᵉʿal are formed from a different root, hwk: יְהָךְ, לִמְהָךְ.

170. *חֲיָה "to live" has the hap̄ʿel *haḥḥī, part. מַחֵא (maḥḥē) D 5:19.

171. כהל, יכל "to be able to, prevail": כהל forms the participle יְכֵלָה, כָּהֵל, כָּהֲלִין. יכל has the perfect יָכֵל, יְכֵלְתְּ, the participle יָכִל, יָכְלָה, יָכְלִין, the imperfect תּוּכַל, יוּכַל, יִכֻּל (tūkal, read tikkul). For yikkul, cf. par. 128; yūkal, probably an ancient hup̄ʿal formation, is commonly used in Hebrew and preserved here in BA.

As in English, כהל, יכל are followed by the infinitive introduced by ל.

172. *סְלִק "to go up." In forms in which סל are not separated by a vowel, ל is assimilated to ס. The resulting ss may be nasalized: pᵉʿal סִלְקַת (rather than סָלְקָת D 7:8), סָלְקָן, סְלִקוּ, but hap̄ʿel לְהַנְסָקָה, הַסִּקוּ, passive הֻסַּק.

173. *אֶשְׁתִּי "to drink" shows prosthetic ᵃi- only in the perfect; cf. the participle שָׁתֵה, שָׁתַיִן, imperfect יִשְׁתּוֹן.

13. The verb with pronominal suffixes

For a listing of all attested forms, cf. the paradigms, p. 71.

174. The forms of the verbal suffixes are the same as those of the noun (par. 31), except for the suffix of the 1. sg. which is נִי- (unstressed). This נִי- is used also with the infinitive: לְהוֹדָעוּתַּנִי "to let me know."

There is no pronominal suffix for the 3. pl., but the seemingly independent personal pronoun הִמּוֹ, הִמּוֹן is used (par. 29).

175. In the imperfect, the suffix is preceded by -(i)nn-: יְהוֹדְעִנַּנִי "he will let me know," יְשֵׁיזְבִנָּךְ "he will save you," יִתְּנִנַּהּ "he gives it

(fem.)." Reduction of $nn > n$ occurs when it is vowelless: יִשְׁאֲלִנְכוֹן
"he will ask you (pl.)" E 7:21, יְשֵׁיזְבִנְכוֹן "he will save you" D 3:15.
In the 3. and 2. masc. pl., -ūn-n was perhaps pronounced -unn-,
with shortened u (par. 10, 147).

In the jussive and the imperative, the suffix is attached directly
to the verb: (לוּךְ-) אַל יְבַהֲלָךְ "let it (them) not frighten you!,"
הַעֲלֹנִי "let me enter!"

176. Slightly different forms result when the suffixes are attached
to roots ending in w/y/ʾ, such as יְחַוִּנַּהּ "he will tell it (fem.)" D 2:11.

14. Notes on the syntax of the verb

177. The participle may indicate the immediate present, for instance: מְהוֹדְעִין אֲנַחְנָה לְמַלְכָּא "we (hereby) inform the king" E 4:16.
This led to the widespread use of the participle to indicate an
action that is simultaneous with the main action. Therefore, the
participle must often be translated by the past tense, for instance:
בַּהּ שַׁעֲתָה נְפַקָה אֶצְבְּעָן ... וְכָתְבָן "at this very moment, fingers ...
came out and wrote" D 5:5.
This led further to the free use of the participle as a narrative
tense, for instance: בֵּאדַיִן מִתְכַּנְּשִׁין אֲחַשְׁדַּרְפְּנַיָּא ... וְקָיְמִין ... וְכָרוֹזָא קָרֵא
"thereupon, the satraps ... assembled ... and stood ... and the
herald called" D 3:3f.
The participle may also be used to indicate continuous and
habitual action, for instance: דִּי קִרְיְתָא דָךְ מִן יוֹמָת עָלְמָא עַל מַלְכִין
מִתְנַשְּׂאָה וּמְרַד וְאֶשְׁתַּדּוּר מִתְעֲבֶד־בַּהּ "that this city has been rising up
against kings since the days of eternity and rebellion and insurrection have (always) occurred in it" E 4:19. However, this mode is
more commonly expressed by הֲוָה "to be" with the participle:
וַהֲוַת בְּטֵלָא "(work on the temple) was idle (all the time)" E 4:24,
הֲוָה בְּנֵה מִקַּדְמַת דְּנָה שְׁנִין שַׂגִּיאָן "(the temple) had been standing built
formerly for many years" E 5:11, כָּל קֳבֵל דִּי הֲוָא עָבֵד מִן קַדְמַת דְּנָה
"as he used to do formerly" D 6:11.

178. Use of the imperfect to indicate simultaneous action
antedates that of the participle. In BA, it occurs rarely: עַיְנַי
לִשְׁמַיָּא נִטְלֵת וּמַנְדְּעִי עֲלַי יְתוּב "I lifted my eyes toward heaven, and
my knowledge returned to me" D 4:31.

The imperfect indicates the past after the conjunction "until" in E 5:5, עַד טַעְמָא לְדָרְיָוֶשׁ יְהָךְ "until Darius' order came."

The unexplained יַחִיטוּ (וְאֻשַּׁיָּא) E 4:12 is occasionally considered an imperfect (jussive?), but it would seem to be a perfect (*yaḥḥiṭū*, root *yḥṭ* < *wḥṭ* = *ḥwṭ* "they have walled the foundations," a gloss to the preceding שַׁכְלִלוּ (וְשׁוּרַיָּא).

179. The perfect is used to indicate the future in D 7:27, וּמַלְכוּתָה ... יְהִיבַת לְעַם קַדִּישֵׁי עֶלְיוֹנִין "the kingdom ... will be given to the people of the holy ones of the Most High." This may be due to the fact that the passive pᵉᶜal was felt to be closely related to the passive participle.

180. The verb of more than one subject may be either sg. or pl., regardless of whether it comes before or after the subjects.

181. The 3. masc. pl. and the masc. pl. of the participle frequently express an impersonal subject and thus substitute for a passive construction: וְלָךְ טָרְדִין מִן אֲנָשָׁא ... וְעִשְׂבָּא כְתוֹרִין לָךְ יְטַעֲמוּן "they (one) will drive you out from mankind ... and will make you eat grass like oxen" = "you will be driven out, etc." D 4:22.

182. The direct object is frequently introduced by the preposition לְ. It may, however, be noted that in BA, a large percentage of these cases concerns the direct object of an infinitive or participle.

183. The position of words in a verbal sentence is free and does not follow any hard and fast rules. The more ancient sequence *verb-subject-object* occurs occasionally, in particular in dependent clauses and after such particles as כְּעַן "now," בֵּאדַיִן "then." Preference is shown to the sequence *object-verb-subject*. In sentences containing no direct object, the preferred sequence is *subject-verb*. Other combinations are possible.

184. The direct object may precede the verb and later in the sentence be referred to by the appropriate pronoun or pronominal suffix: וּבַיְתָה דְנָה סַתְרֵהּ וְעַמָּה הַגְלִי "and he tore down this house and exiled the people" E 5:12, הִמּוֹ (rather *aḥḥet*) אֵלֶּה מָאנַיָּא שֵׂא אֵזֶל אֲחֵת "take these vessels and go and deposit them" E 5:15 (contrast גֻּבְרַיָּא אִלֵּךְ ... קַטִּל הִמּוֹן שְׁבִיבָא E 6:5), וְאַף מָאנֵי בֵית אֱלָהָא ... יַהֲתִיבוּן "a fiery flame killed those men" D 3:22, וּשְׁאָר חֵיוָתָא הֶעְדִּיו דִּי נוּרָא

שְׁלְטָנְהוֹן "and they took away the dominion of all the other animals" D 7:12.

185. The infinitive may follow or precede its object. Examples of both usages occur with about equal frequency.

XIV. The Vocabulary

186. Aramaic has been influenced to an extraordinary degree by the fact that it had to live together with—and was dominated by—a variety of other languages. Its vocabulary shows manifold layers of foreign influence which shed light upon the historical development of the language.

Inner-Aramaic preferences in the choice of words, for dialectal or stylistic reasons, can be observed in BA in the form of glosses that have entered the text: בְּדִתְאָא דִּי בְרָא for בְּעֵשֶׂב אַרְעָא "with the vegetation of the field (earth)" D 4:12 (cf. Gen. 1:11f.), בְּנַגְהָא for בְּשַׁפַרְפָּרָא "at dawn" D 6:20.

A number of Hebrew, Akkadian, and Persian proper names of persons and localities are to be found in BA.

187. Hebrew influence must be assumed for many words of religious significance or words designating Jewish institutions. These may be completely aramaicized and may originally have been common to Aramaic and the Canaanite/Hebrew group, but their existence in BA is due to Jewish influence. Such words are נְבִיאָה "prophet," נְבוּאָה "prophecy," כָּהֲנַיָּא "priests," לֵוָיֵא "Levites," נְתִינַיָּא "temple servants," מִנְחָה "offering," נִיחוֹחִין "sacrifices of sweet smell," נִסְכֵּיהוֹן "their libations," מַלְאַךְ "angel," שִׁבְטֵי יִשְׂרָאֵל "the tribes of Israel" E 6:17, לְחַטָּיָא "to make a sin offering" E 6:17, חַרְטֹם "magician" (of Egyptian origin?). The fact of Hebrew origin is occasionally proven or made likely by phonetic reasons, as in שָׁפְטִין "judges" (par. 18) or עֶלְיוֹנִין "most high" (par. 22).

188. Akkadian influence extended over many centuries and also reflects dialectal distinctions. There are ancient cultural loans, such as הֵיכְלָא "temple, palace" (< ekallu, through Hurrian and Canaanite?), כָּרְסָא "chair" (< kussium, kussū), probably also אַתּוּן "furnace" (< atūnu). Terms such as אַרְגְּוָנָא "purple" (< argaman-nu) and פַּרְזֶל "iron" (< parzillu) entered Aramaic through Akkadian.

5*

The bulk of Akkadian loan words concerns terms of the political and financial administration, such as סְגַן "prefect" (< *šaknu*), פֶּחָה "governor" (< *piḫatu, pāḫatu*), (*כְּנָת) כְּנָה "colleague" (< *kinattu*), הֲלָךְ בְּלוֹ, מִדָּה (מִנְדָּה) for various kinds of taxes (< *ma(n)dattu, biltu, ilku*), נִכְסִין "possessions" (< pl. *nik(k)assū*), אִגְּרָה "letter" (< *egirtu*). Terms for monetary units such as מְנָא "mina" (< *manū*) and פְּרַס "half-mina" or "half-shekel" (< *parsu*) are derived from Akkadian. There are loan translations such as תְּלָתָא "triumvir" (< *šalšu*, par. 71), עֲבַר נַהֲרָא "the Trans-Euphrates Province" (lit., "across-the-river," < *eber nāri*), בְּעֵל טְעֵם "official in charge" (< *bēl ṭēmi*).

Military influence is indicated in בִּירְתָא "fortress" (< *bīrtu*) and, possibly, קְרָב "war" (< *qarābu*?). A legal loan word is זָכוּ "innocence" (< *zakūtu*).

Another group of Akkadian loan words are cultural terms connected with architecture (נִדְבָּךְ "layer" < *nadbaku*, and, possibly, מְסוֹבְלִין [par. 130] < imp. *šubil*); with palace life (שֵׁגְלְתָא "concubines" < **ša ekalli*?); and religious practices (אַשַׁף "enchanter" < *āšipu*).

Finally, there are ordinary words, such as the verbs שֵׁיזִב "to save" (< *ušēzib*), שֵׁיצִי(א) "to complete" (< *ušēṣi*), שַׁכְלֵל "to complete" (< *ušaklil*), possibly also חֲשַׁח "needed, necessary" (from the root *ḫašāḫu*); further, זִיו "facial features" (< pl. *zīmū*). Their acceptance attests to the intimate contact between the two languages.

189. Persian influence shows itself in the sphere of political and legal administration and in the phraseology of written communication. Thus, we find אֲחַשְׁדַּרְפְּנַיָּא "satraps" (< **xšaϑrapāna*, through Akkadian?; OPers. has a different formation, *xšaśapāvā*, and the Greek form presupposes **xšaϑrapā*), אֲדַרְגָּזְרַיָּא "counselors" (?, < **handarza-kara*, Mod. Pers. *andarzǧar*), הַדָּבְרִין "companions" (< **hada-bāra*, MPers. *hadbār*, Mod. Pers. *yār*), סָרְכִין "chief ministers" (< **sāraka*, to Av. *sāra* "head"), גְּדָבְרַיָּא, גִּזְבְּרַיָּא "treasurers," גְּנַזַּיָּא "treasures" (< *ganzabara, ganza*, Mod. Pers. *ganjūr, ganj*), אֲפַרְסַתְכָיֵא "leading officials" (?, < **fra-stā-ka*, corresponding to Greek *prostatēs*?, or to be corrected to אֲפַרְסְכָיֵא < **frasaka* > Akkad. *ip-ra-sak-ka*?), תִּפְתָּיֵא "police chiefs" (< **tāyu-pātā*), דְּתָבְרַיָּא "law officials," דָּת "law" (< *dātabara, dāta*, Mod. Pers. *dāvar, dād*),

שְׁרֹשִׁי "corporal punishment" (par. 19, 57, < *srauśyā, Av. sraośyā), הַדָּמִין "limbs" (< *handāma(n), Mod. Pers. andām) in the legal phrase הַדָּמִין תִּתְעַבְדוּן "you will be dismembered," נִשְׁתְּוָנָא "written order" (< *ni-šta-van, Ossetic nystwan), פַּרְשֶׁגֶן "copy" (פִּתְשֶׁגֶן in a Hebrew context, < *pati-čagna, Armen. patčēn, Pahl. pačēn), פִּתְגָם "message, word" (< *pati-gāma, Mod. Pers. paygām). Cf. also the loan translation מֶלֶךְ מַלְכַיָא "king of kings." Epistolary and documentary style also added some adverbs to the language, such as אָסְפַּרְנָא "exactly, perfectly" (< *asprnā, Av. aspərənah), אַדְרַזְדָּא "diligently" (< *drazdā, Av. zrazdā). Cf. also אַזְדָּא "publicly known" (< azdā).

Cultural terms are represented by words used for various parts of dress: המונכא "necklace" (q'rē הַמְנִיכָא*, הַמְיָנְכָא < *hamyā(ha)naka, Mod. Pers. hamyān "belt"), סַרְבָּלֵיהוֹן "their trousers" (< *sala-vāra, Mod. Pers. šalvār), probably also פַּטִּישֵׁיהוֹן "their shirts" (?) and כַּרְבְּלָתְהוֹן "their hats" (< Akk. karballatu, probably neither a Persian nor an Akkadian word, but a part of Persian dress). A much discussed building term, אֻשַּׁרְנָא "furnishings" (?, < āčarna, MPers. āčār), also appears to be of Persian origin.

Ordinary words, such as רָזָא "secret" (< *rāza, Mod. Pers. rāz) and *זַן "kind" (< zana), also found their way from Persian into Aramaic.

190. A number of words may be suspected of being of Akkadian or Persian origin. אַפְתֹם may be Akk. appittimma and mean "certainly," or Persian *apatama(m), MPers. abdum "finally." Further, אֶשְׁתַּדּוּר "insurrection" (< Pers. *ā(x)šti-drauga "breach of peace," cf. par. 111), נְוָלִי (-לוּ) "dunghill" (Akk.?), נְבִזְבָּה "gift" (par. 62), נֶבְרַשְׁתָּא "lamp" (perhaps < Pers. *ni-brāšti-, to Av. brāz-, Sanskrit bhrāj- "to shine"), נִדְנֶה, probably to be read נִדְנַהּ "its sheath" D 7:15 (< Pers. nidāni "container," in Elamite "storehouse;" cf. nidāman, Mod. Pers. niyām "sheath").

191. Greek loan words belong to the cultural sphere. They are the terms for musical instruments repeatedly mentioned in Daniel ch. 3: קִיתָרֹ(ו)ס (qatṛōs) "kitharis," פְּסַנְטֵרִין (D 3:7) פְּסַנְתֵּרִין "psaltēri(o)n," סִיפֹּנְיָה, סוּמְפֹּנְיָה "symphōnia." Greek origin has been claimed but never been proved for other words. It also remains doubtful whether טַרְפְּלָיֵא E 4:9 may mean "men from Tripolis."

Paradigms

1. The strong verb

Perfect

	pᵃal	pa''el	haṗ'el
sg. 3. masc.	כְּתַב	כַּתֵּב (כַּתֵּב)	הַכְתֵּב (אַכְתֵּב, תֵּב-)
3. fem.	כִּתְבַת	כַּתְּבַת	הַכְתְּבַת
2. masc.	כְּתַבְתְּ (כְּתַֿבְתָּ, ־תָּה)	כַּתֶּבְתְּ	הַכְתֶּבְתְּ
2. fem.	כְּתַֿבְתִּי	כַּתֵּבְתִּי	הַכְתֵּבְתִּי
1.	כִּתְבֵת	כַּתְּבֵת	הַכְתְּבֵת
pl. 3. masc.	כְּתַֿבוּ	כַּתִּֿבוּ	הַכְתִּֿבוּ
3. fem.	כְּתַֿבָה (כתבו *kᵉtib*)	כַּתִּֿבָה	הַכְתִּֿבָה
2. masc.	כְּתַבְתּוּן	כַּתֶּבְתּוּן	הַכְתֶּבְתּוּן
2. fem.	כְּתַבְתֵּן	כַּתֶּבְתֵּן	הַכְתֶּבְתֵּן
1.	כְּתַֿבְנָא	כַּתֵּֿבְנָא	הַכְתֵּֿבְנָא

Imperfect

	pᵃal	pa''el	haṗ'el
sg. 3. masc.	יִכְתֻּב	יְכַתֵּב (־תֵּב)	יְהַכְתֵּב (יְכַתֵּב, ־תֵּב)
3. fem.	תִּכְתֻּב	תְּכַתֵּב	תְּהַכְתֵּב
2. masc.	תִּכְתֻּב	תְּכַתֵּב	תְּהַכְתֵּב
2. fem.	תִּכְתְּבִין	תְּכַתְּבִין	תְּהַכְתְּבִין
1.	אֶכְתֻּב	אֲכַתֵּב	אֲהַכְתֵּב
pl. 3. masc.	יִכְתְּבוּן	יְכַתְּבוּן	יְהַכְתְּבוּן
3. fem.	יִכְתְּבָן	יְכַתְּבָן	יְהַכְתְּבָן
2. masc.	תִּכְתְּבוּן	תְּכַתְּבוּן	תְּהַכְתְּבוּן
2. fem.	תִּכְתְּבָן	תְּכַתְּבָן	תְּהַכְתְּבָן
1.	נִכְתֻּב	נְכַתֵּב	נְהַכְתֵּב

Imperative	pᵊ‘al	pa‘‘el	hap̄‘el
sg. 2. masc.	כְּתֻב	כַּתֵּב (-תֵּב)	הַכְתֵּב (אַכְתֵּב, -תֵּב)
2. fem.	כְּתֻׁבִי	כַּתֵּׁבִי	הַכְתֵּׁבִי
pl. 2. masc.	כְּתֻׁבוּ	כַּתֵּׁבוּ	הַכְתֵּׁבוּ
2. fem.	כְּתֻׁבָה	כַּתֵּׁבָה	הַכְתֵּׁבָה

Infinitive	pᵊ‘al	pa‘‘el	hap̄‘el
	מִכְתַּב	כַּתָּבָה	הַכְתָּבָה (אַכְ-)

Participle	pᵊ‘al		pa‘‘el	
	act.	pass.	act.	pass.
sg. masc.	כָּתֵב (כָּתֵב)	כְּתִיב	מְכַתֵּב (-תֵּב)	מְכַתַּב
fem.	כָּתְבָה	כְּתִיבָה	מְכַתְּבָה	מְכַתְּבָה
pl. masc.	כָּתְבִין	כְּתִיבִין	מְכַתְּבִין	מְכַתְּבִין
fem.	כָּתְבָן	כְּתִיבָן	מְכַתְּבָן	מְכַתְּבָן

	hap̄‘el	
	act.	pass.
sg. masc.	מְהַכְתֵּב (מַכְתֵּב, -תֵּב)	מְהַכְתַּב
fem.	מְהַכְתְּבָה	מְהַכְתְּבָה
pl. masc.	מְהַכְתְּבִין	מְהַכְתְּבִין
fem.	מְהַכְתְּבָן	מְהַכְתְּבָן

Passive Perfect	pᵉʿīl	puʿʿal	hu/oᵖʿal
sg. 3. masc.	כְּתִיב	כְּתֵּב	הֻכְתַּב (הָכְ-)
3. fem.	כְּתִיבַת	כֻּתְּבַת	הֻכְתְּבַת
2. masc.	כְּתִיבְתְּ (-תָּה)	כֻּתַּבְתְּ	הֻכְתַּבְתְּ
2. fem.	כְּתִיבְתִּי	כֻּתַּבְתִּי	הֻכְתַּבְתִּי
1.	כְּתִיבֵת	כֻּתְּבֵת	הֻכְתְּבֵת
pl. 3. masc.	כְּתִיבוּ	כֻּתַּבוּ	הֻכְתַּבוּ
3. fem.	כְּתִיבָה	כֻּתַּבָה	הֻכְתַּבָה
2. masc.	כְּתִיבְתּוּן	כֻּתַּבְתּוּן	הֻכְתַּבְתּוּן
2. fem.	כְּתִיבְתֵּן	כֻּתַּבְתֵּן	הֻכְתַּבְתֵּן
1.	כְּתִיבְנָא	כֻּתַּבְנָא	הֻכְתַּבְנָא

Perfect	hitpᵉʿel	hitpaʿʿal
sg. 3. masc.	הִתְכְּתֵב (אֶתְ-, -תְב)	הִתְכַּתַּב (אֶתְ-)
3. fem.	הִתְכַּתְבַת	הִתְכַּתְּבַת
2. masc.	הִתְכְּתַבְתְּ (-תֵּבְתְּ)	הִתְכַּתַּבְתְּ
2. fem.	הִתְכְּתַבְתִּי	הִתְכַּתַּבְתִּי
1.	הִתְכְּתְבֵת	הִתְכַּתְּבֵת
pl. 3. masc.	הִתְכַּתְּבוּ	הִתְכַּתַּבוּ
3. fem.	הִתְכַּתְּבָה	הִתְכַּתַּבָה
2. masc.	הִתְכְּתַבְתּוּן	הִתְכַּתַּבְתּוּן
2. fem.	הִתְכְּתַבְתֵּן	הִתְכַּתַּבְתֵּן
1.	הִתְכְּתַבְנָא	הִתְכַּתַּבְנָא

Imperfect	hitpᵉᶜel	hitpaᶜᶜal
sg. 3. masc.	יִתְכְּתֵב (תְּב-)	יִתְכַּתַּב
3. fem.	תִּתְכְּתֵב	תִּתְכַּתַּב
2. masc.	תִּתְכְּתֵב	תִּתְכַּתַּב
2. fem.	תִּתְכַּתְבִין	תִּתְכַּתְּבִין
1.	אֶתְכְּתֵב	אֶתְכַּתַּב
pl. 3. masc.	יִתְכַּתְבוּן	יִתְכַּתְּבוּן
3. fem.	יִתְכַּתְבָן	יִתְכַּתְּבָן
2. masc.	תִּתְכַּתְבוּן	תִּתְכַּתְּבוּן
2. fem.	תִּתְכַּתְבָן	תִּתְכַּתְּבָן
1.	נִתְכְּתֵב	נִתְכַּתַּב

Infinitive	הִתְכְּתָבָה (אֶת-)	הִתְכַּתָּבָה (אֶת-)

Participle		
sg. masc.	מִתְכְּתֵב (תְּב-)	מִתְכַּתַּב
fem.	מִתְכַּתְבָה	מִתְכַּתְּבָה
pl. masc.	מִתְכַּתְבִין	מִתְכַּתְּבִין
fem.	מִתְכַּתְבָן	מִתְכַּתְּבָן

2. Roots with ו or י as the second consonant

Perfect	pᵃʿal	hap̄ʿel	hitp̄ᵃʿel
sg. 3. masc.	קָם (שָׂם, רָם)	הֲקֵים (הֲקֵים, אֲקֵים)	
3. fem.	קָמַת	הֲקֵימַת	
2. masc.	קָמְתְּ	הֲקֵימְתְּ	
2. fem.	קָמְתִּי	הֲקֵימְתִּי	
1.	קָמֵת	הֲקֵימֵת	
pl. 3. masc.	קָמוּ	הֲקֵימוּ	
3. fem.	קָמָה	הֲקֵימָה	
2. masc.	קָמְתּוּן	הֲקֵימְתּוּן	
2. fem.	קָמְתֵּן	הֲקֵימְתֵּן	
1.	קָמְנָא	הֲקֵימְנָא	

Imperfect	pᵃʿal	hap̄ʿel	hitp̄ᵃʿel
sg. 3. masc.	יְקוּם (יְשִׂים)	יְקֵים, יְהָקֵים	יִתְּזָן, יִתְּשָׂם
3. fem.	תְּקוּם	תְּקֵים (תָּסִיף)	
2. masc.	תְּקוּם	תְּקֵים	
2. fem.	תְּקוּמִין	תְּקֵימִין	
1.	אֲקוּם	אֲקֵים	
pl. 3. masc.	יְקוּמוּן	יְקֵימוּן (יְהָקֵימוּן)	יִתְּשָׂמוּן
3. fem.	יְקוּמָן	יְקֵימָן	
2. masc.	תְּקוּמוּן	תְּקֵימוּן	
2. fem.	תְּקוּמָן	תְּקֵימָן	
1.	נְקוּם	נְקֵים	

Imperative	pᵃ‹al	hap̄‹el	hitpᵃ‹el
sg. 2. masc.	קוּם (שִׂים)	הָקִים	
2. fem.	קוּמִי (שִׂימִי)	הָקִימִי	
pl. 2. masc.	קוּמוּ (שִׂימוּ)	הָקִימוּ	
2. fem.	קוּמָה (שִׂימָה)	הָקִימָה	

Infinitive	מְקָם	הֲקָמָה	הִתְּקָמָה

Participle	act.	pass.	act.	pass.	
sg. masc.	קָאֵם	שִׂים	מְהָקִים	מְקָם (?)	מִתְּשָׂם
			(מָקִים, מְקִים)		
fem.	קָיְמָה (קאמה)	שִׂימָה	מְקִימָה		מִתְּשָׂמָה
pl. masc.	קָיְמִין (קאמין)	שִׂימִין	מְקִימִין		מִתְּשָׂמִין
fem.	קָיְמָן (קאמן)	שִׂימָן	מְקִימָן		מִתְּשָׂמָן

Passive Perfect	pᵃ‹īl	hu/op̄‹al
sg. 3. masc.	שִׂים (?)	
3. fem.	שָׂמַת	הֲקִימַת (הֲקָמַת?)

3. Roots ending in י/ו or א

Perfect

		pᵊʿal	paʿʿel	hapʿel
sg. 3. masc.	(אֶשְׁתִּי)	בְּנָה	בַּנִּי	הַבְנִי
3. fem.	(אֶשְׁתִּיַת ؟)	בְּנָת	בַּנִּית (؟)	הַבְנִית (؟)
2. masc.	(אֶשְׁתִּ֫יַת)	בְּנַ֫יִת	בַּנִּ֫ית	הַבְנִ֫ית
2. fem.	(אֶשְׁתִּ֫יַתִי)	בְּנַ֫יִתִי	בַּנִּיתִי	הַבְנִיתִי
1.	(אֶשְׁתִּית)	בְּנֵית	בַּנִּית	הַבְנִית
pl. 3. masc.	(אֶשְׁתִּיו)	בְּנוֹ	בַּנִּיו	הַבְנִיו
3. fem.	(אֶשְׁתִּ֫יָה ؟)	בְּנָה (؟)	בַּנִּ֫יָה (؟)	הַבְנִ֫יָה (؟)
2. masc.	(אֶשְׁתִּיתון)	בְּנֵיתון	בַּנִּיתון	הַבְנִיתון
2. fem.	(אֶשְׁתִּיתֵן)	בְּנֵיתֵן	בַּנִּיתֵן	הַבְנִיתֵן
1.	(אֶשְׁתִּ֫ינָא)	בְּנֵ֫ינָא	בַּנִּ֫ינָא	הַבְנִ֫ינָא

Imperfect

	pᵊʿal	paʿʿel	hapʿel
sg. 3. masc.	יִבְנֵא	יְבַנֵּא	יְהַבְנֵא (יִבְנֵא)
3. fem.	תִּבְנֵא	תְּבַנֵּא	תְּהַבְנֵא
2. masc.	תִּבְנֵא	תְּבַנֵּא	תְּהַבְנֵא
2. fem.	תִּבְנֵין (؟)	תְּבַנֵּין (؟)	תְּהַבְנֵין (؟)
1.	אֶבְנֵא	אֲבַנֵּא	אֲהַבְנֵא
pl. 3. masc.	יִבְנוֹן	יְבַנּוֹן	יְהַבְנוֹן
3. fem.	יִבְנְיָן	יְבַנְּיָן	יְהַבְנְיָן
2. masc.	תִּבְנוֹן	תְּבַנּוֹן	תְּהַבְנוֹן
2. fem.	תִּבְנְיָן	תְּבַנְּיָן	תְּהַבְנְיָן
1.	נִבְנֵא	נְבַנֵּא	נְהַבְנֵא

Imperative	pᵉʿal	paʿʿel	hap̄ʿel
sg. 2. masc.	בְּנִי	בַּנִּי (מַּנִּי)	הַבְנִי
2. fem.			
pl. 2. masc.	בְּנוֹ	בַּנּוֹ	הַבְנוֹ
2. fem.			

Infinitive	מִבְנָא	בַּנָּיָה	הַבְנָיָה

Participle	pᵉʿal		paʿʿel		hap̄ʿel	
	act.	pass.	act.	pass.	act.	pass.
sg. masc.	בָּנֵה (-א)	בְּנֵה (-א)	מְבַנֵּי (?)	מְבַנָּא	מְהַבְנֵי (?)	מְהַבְנָא (מַבְנָא)
fem.	בַּנְיָה	בַּנְיָה	מְבַנְיָה	מְבַנְיָה	מְהַבְנְיָה	מְהַבְנְיָה
pl. masc.	בָּנַיִן	בְּנַיִן	מְבַנְּיַן	מְבַנְּיַן	מְהַבְנַיִן	מְהַבְנַיִן
fem.	בַּנְיָן	בַּנְיָן	מְבַנְיָן	מְבַנְיָן	מְהַבְנְיָן	מְהַבְנְיָן

Passive Perfect		
sg. 3. masc.	בְּנִי	
3. fem.		הֵיתָיִת
pl. 3. masc.	בְּנִיו	הֵיתָיִו

Perfect	hitpᵉʿel	hitpaʿʿal
sg. 3. masc.	הִתְבְּנִי (אֶתְ-)	הִתְבְּנִי (אֶתְ-)
3. fem.	הִתְבַּנִּית	הִתְבַּנִּית (?)
2. masc.	הִתְבְּנִיתָ	הִתְבְּנִיתָ
2. fem.	הִתְבְּנִיתִי	הִתְבְּנִיתִי
1.	הִתְבְּנִית	הִתְבְּנִית
pl. 3. masc.	הִתְבְּנִיו	הִתְבְּנִיו
3. fem.	הִתְבְּנִיָה (?)	הִתְבְּנִיָה (?)
2. masc.	הִתְבְּנִיתוּן	הִתְבְּנִיתוּן
2. fem.	הִתְבְּנִיתֶן	הִתְבְּנִיתֶן
1.	הִתְבְּנִינָא	הִתְבְּנִינָא

Imperfect		
sg. 3. masc.	יִתְבְּנֵא	יִתְבְּנֵא
3. fem.	תִּתְבְּנֵא	תִּתְבְּנֵא
2. masc.	תִּתְבְּנֵא	תִּתְבְּנֵא
2. fem.	תִּתְבְּנֵין (?)	תִּתְבְּנֵין (?)
1.	אֶתְבְּנֵא	אֶתְבְּנֵא
pl. 3. masc.	יִתְבְּנוֹן	יִתְבְּנוֹן
3. fem.	יִתְבְּנֵין	יִתְבְּנֵין
2. masc.	תִּתְבְּנוֹן	תִּתְבְּנוֹן
2. fem.	תִּתְבְּנֵין	תִּתְבְּנֵין
1.	נִתְבְּנֵא	נִתְבְּנֵא

Infinitive	הִתְבְּנָיָה	הִתְבְּנָיָה

Participle		
sg. masc.	מִתְבְּנֵא	מִתְבְּנֵא
fem.	מִתְבַּנְיָה	מִתְבַּנְיָה
pl. masc.	מִתְבְּנַן	מִתְבְּנַן
fem.	מִתְבַּנְיָן	מִתְבַּנְיָן

4. Roots with identical second and third consonants

Perfect	pᵉal	hap̄ᵉel	hu/op̄ᵉal
sg. 3. masc.	עַל	הַעֵל (הַנְעֵל, אַ-)	הֻעַל
3. fem.	עַלַּת (נַדַּת)	הַעֶלֶת	
2. masc.	עַלְלְתְּ	הַעֶלְתְּ	
2. fem.	עֲלַלְתִּי	הַעֶלְתִּי	
1.	עַלְלֵת	הַעֶלֶת	
pl. 3. masc.	עַלּוּ	הַעֵלּוּ	הֻעַלּוּ
3. fem.	עַלָּה	הַעֶלָּה	
2. masc.	עֲלַלְתּוּן	הַעֶלְתּוּן	
2. fem.	עֲלַלְתֵּן	הַעֶלְתֵּן	
1.	עֲלַלְנָא	הַעֶלְנָא	

Imperfect			
sg. 3. masc.	יֵעַל	יְהַעֵל (יֵעַל)	
3. fem.	תֵּעַל	תְּהַעֵל	
2. masc.	תֵּעַל	תְּהַעֵל	
2. fem.	תֵּעֲלִין	תְּהַעֲלִין	
1.	אֵעַל	אֲהַעֵל	
pl. 3. masc.	יֵעֲלוּן	יְהַעֲלוּן	
3. fem.	יֵעֲלָן	יְהַעֲלָן	
2. masc.	תֵּעֲלוּן	תְּהַעֲלוּן	
2. fem.	תֵּעֲלָן	תְּהַעֲלָן	
1.	נֵעַל	נְהַעֵל	

Imperative	pᵉʿal	haₚ̄ᵉel
sg. 2. masc.	עַל	הַעֵל (הַנְעֵל, אַ-)
2. fem.	עֹֹלִּי	הַעֵֹלִּי
pl. 2. masc.	עֹֹלּוּ	הַעֵֹלּוּ
2. fem.	עֹֹלָּה	הַעֵֹלָּה

Infinitive	pᵉʿal	haₚ̄ᵉel
	מֵעַל	הֶעָלָה (הַנְעָלָה)

Participle	pᵉʿal		haₚ̄ᵉel	
	act.	pass.	act.	pass.
sg. masc.	עָלֵל	עֲלִיל	מְהַעֵל (מַעֵל)	מְהַעַל (מַעַל)
fem.	עָלְלָה		מְהַעְלָה	
pl. masc.	עָלְלִין		מְהַעֲלִין	
fem.	עָלְלָן		מְהַעֲלָן	

5. Verbs with pronominal suffixes

Perfect   Imperative

	Perfect sg. 3.masc.	Perfect sg. 2.masc.	Perfect 1.	Perfect pl. 3.masc.	Imperative sg. 2.masc.	Imperative pl. 2.masc.
suffix sg. 1.		הוֹדַעְתַּנִי		חַבְּלוּנִי	הַעֵלְנִי	הַחֲוֹנִי
2. masc.	הוֹדְעָךְ הַשְׁלְטָךְ					
3. masc.	סַתְרֵהּ שַׁכְלְלֵהּ שָׂמֵהּ בַּנְהִי הַשְׁלְטֵהּ הֲקִימֵהּ (אֲקִימֵהּ)			הַקְרְבֻוֹהִי שָׁנֻּוֹהִי		חַבְּלוּהִי
3. fem.	חַתְמַהּ הַשְׁלְמַהּ		בְּנַיְתַהּ			
pl. 1.		הוֹדַעְתֶּנָא		הֵתִיבֻֿונָא		

Imperfect

	sg. 3.masc.	sg. 3.fem.	sg. 1.	pl. 3.masc.	pl. 2.masc.
suffix sg.1.	יְדַחֲלֻנַּנִי יְהוֹדְעַנִּי יְחַוֻּנַּנִי			יְהוֹדְעֻנַּנִי יְבַהֲלֻונַּנִי (-לַנִּי)	תְּהוֹדְעֻנַּנִי (-עַנַּנִי) תְּהַחֲוֻנַּנִי
2.masc.	יְשֵׁיזְבִנָּךְ יְבַהֲלָךְ (jussive)			יְבַהֲלֻוךְ (jussive)	
3.masc.			אֲהוֹדְעִנֵּהּ	יְשַׁמְּשֻׁונֵּהּ יְבַהֲלֻונֵּהּ (-לַנֵּהּ) יְטַעֲמֻונֵּהּ	
3.fem.	יִתְנִנַּהּ יְחֻוִּנַּהּ	תְּדֻושִׁנַּהּ תְּדִקְנַּהּ			
pl.2.masc.	יִשְׁאֲלֶנְכֹון יְשֵׁיזְבִנְכֹון				

Short Bibliography

(a) General Studies on Aramaic

Baumgartner (W.), *Das Aramäische im Buche Daniel*, in *Zeitschrift für die Alttestamentliche Wissenschaft*, N.F. IV (1927), 81—133. Reprinted in his *Zum Alten Testament und seiner Umwelt* (Leiden, 1959), 68—123.

Blau (J.), *On Pseudo-Corrections in Some Semitic Languages* (Jerusalem, 1970).

Cross (F. M.) and Freedman (D. N.), *Early Hebrew Orthography* (New Haven, 1952. *American Oriental Series*, XXXVI).

Degen (R.), *Altaramäische Grammatik* (Wiesbaden, 1969. *Abhandlungen für die Kunde des Morgenlandes*, XXXVIII, 3).

Dupont-Sommer (A.), *Les Araméens* (Paris, 1949).

Fitzmyer (J. A.), *The Genesis Apocryphon*, 2nd ed. (Rome, 1971).

Garbini (G.), *Il Semitico di Nord-Ovest* (Naples, 1960).

Ginsberg (H. L.), *Notes on Some Old Aramaic Texts*, in *Journal of Near Eastern Studies*, XVIII (1959), 143—149.

Koopmans (J. J.), *Aramäische Chrestomathie, Ausgewählte Texte (Inschriften, Ostraka, Papyri)* (Leiden, 1962).

Kutscher (E. Y.), *The Language of the Genesis Apocryphon*, in *Scripta Hierosolymitana*, IV (1957), 1—35.

—, *Aramaic*, in *Current Trends in Linguistics*, VI, 347—412 (The Hague, 1970).

Mazar (B.), *The Aramean Empire and its Relations with Israel*, in *The Biblical Archaeologist*, XXV (1962), 98—120.

Morag (S.), *The Vocalization Systems of Arabic, Hebrew, and Aramaic* (The Hague, 1962, 1972).

Moscati (S.), *Sulle origini degli Aramei*, in *Rivista degli Studi Orientali*, XXVI (1951), 16—22.

Naveh (J.), *The Development of the Aramaic Script* (Jerusalem, 1970. *Proceedings of the Israel Academy of Sciences and Humanities*, V, 1).

Rosenthal (F.), *Die aramaistische Forschung seit Th. Nöldeke's Veröffentlichungen* (Leiden, 1939).

— (ed.), *An Aramaic Handbook* (Wiesbaden, 1967).

Rowley (H. H.), *The Aramaic of the Old Testament* (Oxford, 1929).

Soden (W. von), *Aramäische Wörter in neuassyrischen und neu- und spätbabylonischen Texten*, in *Orientalia*, N. S., XXXV (1966), 1—20, XXXVII (1968), 261—271.

Teixidor (J.), *Bulletin d'épigraphie sémitique*, in *Syria*, XLIV (1967), 163—
195, XLV (1968), 353—389, XLVI (1969), 319—358, XLVII (1970),
357—389, XLVIII (1971), 453—493.

Wagner (M.), *Die lexikalischen und grammatikalischen Aramaismen im alt-
testamentlichen Hebräisch* (Berlin, 1966. *Beihefte zur Zeitschrift für die
Alttestamentliche Wissenschaft*, XCVI).

(b) Studies and Commentaries on the Aramaic Texts of the Bible

Charles (R. H.), *A Critical and Exegetical Commentary on the Book of Daniel*
(Oxford, 1929).

Delcor (M.), *Le livre de Daniel* (Paris, 1971).

Ginsberg (H. L.), *Studies in Daniel* (New York, 1948).

Mertens (A.), *Das Buch Daniel im Lichte der Texte vom Toten Meer* (Würz-
burg, 1971. *Stuttgarter Biblische Monographien*, XII).

Montgomery (J. A.), *The Book of Daniel* (New York, 1927).

Myers (J. M.), *Ezra-Nehemia* (New York, 1965).

Rudolph (W.), *Esra und Nehemia* (Tübingen, 1948).

(c) BA Grammars and Grammatical Studies

Bauer (H.) and Leander (P.), *Grammatik des Biblisch-Aramäischen* (Halle,
1927). Also, *Kurzgefaßte Biblisch-Aramäische Grammatik* (Halle, 1929).

Blake (F. R.), *A Resurvey of Hebrew Tenses, with an appendix: Hebrew Influence on Biblical Aramaic* (Rome, 1951. *Scripta Pontificii Instituti
Biblici*, CIII).

—, *Studies in Semitic Grammar V*, in *Journal of the American Oriental
Society*, LXXIII (1953), 7—16.

Carmignac (J.), *Un aramaïsme biblique et qumrânien: L'infinitif placé après
son complément d'objet*, in *Revue de Qumran*, V (1964—66), 503—520.

Dammron (A.), *Grammaire de l'araméen biblique* (Strasbourg, 1961).

Fitzmyer (J. A.), *The Syntax of kl, kl' in the Aramaic Texts from Egypt and in
Biblical Aramaic*, in *Biblica*, XXXVIII (1957), 170—184.

Johns (A. F.), *A Short Grammar of Biblical Aramaic* (Berrien Springs,
Michigan, 1963, 1966).

Kaddari (M. Z.), *Construct State and dī-Phrases in Imperial Aramaic*, in
*Proceedings of the International Conference on Semitic Studies, Jerusalem,
1965*, 102—115 (Jerusalem, 1969).

Marti (K.), *Kurzgefaßte Grammatik der Biblisch-Aramäischen Sprache* (Berlin,
1896, 1911, 1925. *Porta Linguarum Orientalium*).

Morag (S.), *Biblical Aramaic in Geonic Babylonia*, in *Studies in Egyptology
and Linguistics in Honour of H. J. Polotsky*, 117—131 (Jerusalem,
1964).

Muraoka (T.), *Notes on the Syntax of Biblical Aramaic*, in *Journal of Semitic Studies*, XI (1966), 151—167.

Rosén (H. B.), *On the Use of the Tenses in the Aramaic of Daniel*, in *Journal of Semitic Studies*, VI (1961), 183—203.

Schaeder (H. H.), *Iranische Beiträge* I, in *Schriften der Königsberger Gelehrten Gesellschaft, geisteswiss. Kl.*, VI (1930), ·199—296.

Spitaler (A.), *Zur Frage der Geminatendissimilation im Semitischen*, in *Indogermanische Forschungen*, LXI (1952—54), 257—266.

Strack (H. L.), *Grammatik des Biblisch-Aramäischen*, 6th ed. (Munich, 1921).

(d) BA Dictionaries and Lexicographical Studies

Berger (P.-R.), *Zu den Namen Ššbṣr und Šn'ṣr*, in *Zeitschrift für die Alttestamentliche Wissenschaft*, LXXXIII (1971), 98—100.

Bowman (R. A.), *'eben gᵉlāl-aban galâlu*, in *Dōrōn: Hebraic Studies (Essays in Honor of A. I. Katsh)*, 64—74 (New York, 1965).

Eilers (W.), *Iranisches Beamtentum in der keilinschriftlichen Überlieferung*, in *Abhandlungen für die Kunde des Morgenlandes*, XXV (1940).

Ginsberg (H. L.), *Biblical Aramaic*, in Rosenthal (F.), *An Aramaic Handbook* (Wiesbaden, 1967), I/1, 17—39, I/2, 16—41.

Koehler (L.) and Baumgartner (W.), *Lexicon in Veteris Testamenti Libros* (Leiden, 1948—53), 1045—1138 (Aramaic section by Baumgartner); *Supplementum* (Leiden, 1958), 195—208.

Mowinckel (S.), *Uššarnâ*, in *Studia Theologica*, XIX (1965), 130—135.

Rundgren (F.), *Zur Bedeutung von šršw-Ezra VII 26*, in *Vetus Testamentum*, VII (1957), 400—404.

Shaffer (A.), *Hurrian *kirezzi, West-Semitic krz*, in *Orientalia, N. S.*, XXXIV (1965), 32—34.

Vogt (E.), *Lexicon linguae aramaicae Veteris Testamenti documentis antiquis illustratum* (Rome, 1971).

(e) Principal Editions of Aramaic Texts from Egypt[1]

Aimé-Giron (N.), *Adversaria Semitica*, in *Bulletin de l'Institut français d'archéologie orientale*, XXXVIII (1939), 1—63.

Bauer (H.) and Meissner (B.), *Ein aramäischer Pachtvertrag aus dem 7. Jahre Darius I.* (Berlin, 1936. *Sitzungsberichte d. Preuß. Akad. d. Wiss., phil.-hist. Kl.*).

---

[1] For papyri from the Achaemenid period found in Palestine, cf. Cross (F. M.), in *The Biblical Archaeologist*, XXVI (1963), 110—121, and in D. N. Freedman - J. C. Greenfield (eds.), *New Directions in Biblical Archaeology*, 41—62 (Garden City, N. Y., 1969). For later Aramaic texts from the Dead Sea region, cf. the few references above, under (a) and (b).

Bresciani (E.), *Un papiro aramaico da El Hibeh del Museo Archeologico di Firenze*, in *Aegyptus*, XXXIX (1959), 3—8.

—, *Papiri aramaici egiziani di epoca persiana presso il Museo Civico di Padova*, in *Rivista degli Studi Orientali*, XXXV (1960), 11—24.

—, *Un papiro aramaico di età tolemaica*, in *Rendiconti, Accad. Naz. dei Lincei, Classe di scienze mor., stor. e filol.*, VIII, XVII, 5—6 (Rome, 1962), 258—264.

— and Kamil (M.), *Le lettere aramaiche di Hermopoli*, in *Atti* . . ., VIII, XII, 5 (Rome, 1966), 359—428.

Cowley (A.), *Aramaic Papyri of the Fifth Century B. C.* (Oxford, 1923).

Degen (R.), *Ein neuer aramäischer Papyrus aus Elephantine*, in *Neue Ephemeris für Semitische Epigraphik*, I (1972), 9—22.

Driver (G. R.), *Aramaic Documents of the Fifth Century B. C.* (Oxford, 1954). Also, *Abridged and Revised Ed.* (Oxford, 1957).

Dupont-Sommer (A.), *Un papyrus araméen d'époque saïte découvert à Saqqarah*, in *Semitica*, I (1948), 43—68. Cf. Ginsberg (H. L.), in *Bulletin of the American Schools of Oriental Research*, CXL (1948), 24—27.

Grelot (P.), *Documents araméens d'Égypte* (Paris, 1972).

Kraeling (E. G.), *The Brooklyn Museum Papyri* (New Haven, 1953).

Rabinowitz (I.), *Aramaic Inscriptions of the Fifth Century B. C. E. from a North-Arab Shrine in Egypt*, in *Journal of Near Eastern Studies*, XV (1956), 1—9, also XVIII (1959), 154f.

(f) Grammars and Dictionaries for the Texts from Egypt and Other Official Aramaic Material

Jean (C.-F.) and Hoftijzer (J.), *Dictionnaire des inscriptions sémitiques de l'Ouest* (Leiden, 1965).

Leander (P.), *Laut- und Formenlehre des Ägyptisch-Aramäischen* (Göteborg, 1928).

Vinnikov (I. N.), *Slovař arameyskikh nadpisey*, in *Palestinskiy Sbornik*, III (66) (1958), 171—216, IV (67) (1959), 169—240, VII (70) (1962), 192—237 IX (72) (1962), 141—158, XI (74) (1963), 189—232, XIII (76) (1965), 217—262.

Glossary

The numbers found after individual entries refer to the paragraphs where a given root or word is cited. Italicized numbers indicate the more important occurrences.

In the abs. st. of some nouns, it is uncertain whether the last syllable had *a* or *ę*. In these cases, the last syllable is left unvocalized. In a very few other nouns, vowels are also omitted because of uncertainty as to their correct form.

Verbal roots are left entirely unvocalized. *ę/i* indicates the pᵉᶜę/il. *Hitp.*, *pa.*, *hitpa.*, and *hap̄.* stand, respectively, for (h)itpᵉᶜel, paᶜᶜel, (h)itpaᶜᶜal, and (h)ap̄ᶜel. The distinction between *h* or the glottal stop as preformative has been disregarded.

* denotes merely that the *exact* form of a word thus marked does not occur in BA.

א

אַב*	father, *pl.* *אֲבָהָן (26, 49, *62*).
אֵב*	(*suff.* אִנְבֵּהּ) fruit.
אבד	to perish; *hap̄.* to destroy (26, *108, 121, 124*).
אֶבֶן	stone (26, 46, *59*).
אִגְּרָה	(*det.* אִגַּרְתָּא) letter (46, 188).
אֱדַיִן, בֵּאדַיִן	then, thereupon (10, 13, 17, *75, 85, 89*, 177, 183).
אֲדָר	Adar (*month*) (74).
אִדַּר*	threshing floor.
אֲדַרְגָּזֵר*	counselor (*189*).
אַדְרַזְדָּא	diligently (*93, 189*).
אֶדְרָע	arm, might (17).
אָזְדָּא	publicly known, known as decided (86, *93, 189*).
אזה	to heat (10, 13, 88, *121, 123, 149*).
אזל	to go (79, *122*, 184).
אָח*	brother, colleague (10, *62*).
אֲחִידָה*	riddle (111).
אַחְמְתָא	Ecbatana (*OPers. Hagmatāna*).
אַחֲרִי	after (*prep.*) (*84*).
אַחֲרִי*	end (*57*).
אָחֳרִי	*see* אָחֳרָן.
אָחֳרֵין	(···עַד) eventually (*89*).

אָחֳרָן   (*fem.* אָחֳרִי) other (10, *57, 97*).
אֲחַשְׁדַּרְפַּן* satrap (177, *189*).
אִילָן   tree.
אֵימְתָן*   (*fem.* אֵימְתָנִי) frightful (15, *57*).
אִיתַי   to exist, to be (49, 80, 86, *95*).
אֲכַל   to eat (26, *122*).
אַל   not (*87*, 108, 152, 175).
אֵלֶה, אֵלֶּה these (10, 26, *32, 34*, 184).
אֱלָה   god (13, 30, 36, 46—48, *49, 75*, 80, 83, 84, *85*, 184).
אֲלוּ   behold (*91*).
אִלֵּן, אִלֵּין these (*32, 34*).
אִלֵּךְ   those (*32*, 184).
אֲלַף   thousand (42, *51, 63, 68*).
אַמָּה*   (*pl.* אַמִּין) cubit (*61*).
אֻמָּה   (*pl.* *אֻמִּין) nation (23, *61*).
אמן   *hap.* (הֵימִן) to trust, *part. pass.* trusted, trustworthy (*124*).
אמר   to say, to speak, to tell, to command (10, 13, 24, 27, *115, 117, 120, 121, 122*).
אִמַּר*   lamb (79).
אִנְבֵּה   *see* *אֵב.
אֲנָה   I (26, *29*, 36, 88, 91).
אִנּוּן   they, them, those (*29, 30, 32, 38*).
אֱנוֹשׁ* *see* אֲנָשׁ.
אֲנַחְנָה, אֲנַחְנָא we (26, *29*, 30, 177).
אִנִּין   they (*fem.*) (*29, 30*).
אנס   to subdue, to be too difficult for.
אַנַף*   (*dual/pl.*) face.
אֱנָשׁ, אֱנַשׁ (*det.* אֱנָשָׁא) man, someone, men, mankind, human kind, people (*22*, 42, 181).
אַנְתָּה, אַנְתְּ you (*sg. masc.*) (*12, 29*, 30, 36).
אַנְתָּה* (*pl. suff.* נְשַׁיהוֹן) wife (*62*).
אַנְתּוּן you (*pl. masc.*) (*29*).
אֱסוּר   fetter, (*pl.*) imprisonment (75, 86).
אָסְנַפַּר *to be corrected to* אס)רב)נפר Assurbanipal.
אָסְפַּרְנָא exactly, perfectly (26, *93, 189*).
אֱסָר   interdict, prohibition.
אָע   wood, timber, beam (*17*).

אַף   also (*93*, 184).

אֲפַרְסִי*   Persian (*?*) *E 4: 9.*

אֲפַרְסְכִי*   Persian (*?*) *E 5: 6* (*189*).

אֲפַרְסַתְכִי*   magistrate (*?*) (*58*, *189*).

אַפְתֹם   certainly *or* finally (*93*, *190*).

אֶצְבַּע*   finger, toe (*59*, *60*, 177).

אַרְבַּע   four (30, *59*, *63*).

אַרְגְּוָן*   purple (*188*).

אֲרוּ   behold (*91*).

אֹרַח*   (*pl.* אָרְחָן*) way (10, *51*, *60*, 84).

אַרְיֵה   (*pl.* אַרְיָוָן*) lion (48, *54*, 84).

אַרְיוֹךְ   Arioch (*probably Persian*).

אֲרִיךְ   proper (< *OPers.* aryaka?).

אַרְכֻּבָּה*   knee.

אַרְכָה   (long) duration.

אַרְכְּוָי*   man from Uruk, Erechite.

אֲרַע*   earth (17, *59*, 87, 186).

אַרְעָא   lower, inferior (*adv.*) (80, *88*).

אַרְעִי*   bottom (*57*).

אַרְק*   earth (*17*).

אַרְתַּחְשַׁשְׁתְּא   (אַרְתַּחְשַׁסְתְּא) Artaxerxes (< *OPers. Artaxšaśa, with Aramaic ś/st for the peculiar OPers. ś < ϑr*) (19, 79).

אֹשׁ*   (*pl.* אֻשִּׁין*) foundation (178).

אִשָּׁה*, אֶשָּׁא   fire.

אָשַׁף   enchanter (*53*, *188*).

אַשְׁרְנָא   furnishings (*?*) (*189*).

אֶשְׁתַּדּוּר   insurrection (*111*, 177, *190*).

אֶשְׁתִּי*   *see* שׁתה.

אָת*   sign, miracle (92).

אתה   to come; *hap.* (הַיְתִי) to bring (13, 15, 85, *124*, *148*, *151*, [167).

אַתּוּן   furnace (*188*).   [167).

אֲתַר   place, trace (*?*, *D 2: 35*); אֲתַר דִּי there where; בָּאתַר *see* בָּאתַר (*52*, 84, *91*).

ב

בְּ   in, through, with (16, 27, 36, 62, *75*, 76, *77*, 80, 84, 86, 89, 90, 95, 177, 186).

בֵּאדַיִן   *see* אֱדַיִן.

בְּאִישׁ*   bad, evil (13, 15).

בְּאֵשׁ   (ẹ/i) to be evil, (בְּאֵשׁ עֲלוֹהִי) it grieved him (13, 82, 125).

בָּאתַר‎, בָּתַר   after (prep.) (13, 84).

בָּבֶל   Babylon (16, 26, 30, 48, 59).

בַּבְלִי*   Babylonian (58).

בדר   pa. to scatter (115).

בְּהִילוּ   haste (56).

בהל   hitp. to hurry; pa. to disturb; hitpa. to be disturbed (20, 88, 108, 175).

בּוֹזְנַי   see שְׁתַר בּוֹזְנַי.

בטל   (ẹ/i) to be idle; pa. to cause to be idle, to stop some-one from working (10, 23, 102, 177).

בֵּין   (suff. בֵּינֵיהֶן) between (prep.) (49, 84).

בִּינָה   discernment.

בִּירָה*   fortress, (fortified) city (15, 188).

בית   to spend the night (133).

בַּיִת*   (pl. suff. בָּתֵּיכוֹן) house (15, 17, 36, 46, 47, 48, 51, 62, 79, 80, 184).

בָּל   mind (82).

בֵּלְאשַׁצַּר   see בֵּלְשַׁאצַּר.

בלה   pa. to wear out.

בְּלוֹ   a kind of taxes, tribute (188).

בֵּלְטְשַׁאצַּר   Belteshazzar (13, 36).

בֵּלְשַׁאצַּר   Belshazzar (13).

בנה   to build, to rebuild; hitp. to be built (rebuilt) (10, 36, 54, 79, 87, 111, 149, 150, 177).

בִּנְיָן*   building (34).

בנס   to become enraged.

בעה   to search, to seek, to ask, to pray; pa. to search (17).

בָּעוּ   request, prayer (55).

בְּעֵל   master, (בְּעֵל טְעֵם) official in charge (10, 17, 51, 188).

בִּקְעָה*   plain (51).

בקר   pa. to search, to investigate; hitpa. to be searched, investigated (76).

בַּר   (pl. *בְּנִין) son, (בַּר אֱלָהִין) a divine being, (בְּנֵי אֲנָשָׁא) human beings, (בְּנֵי תוֹרִין) young oxen (47, 62, 74, 78, 80).

בַּר*   (*det.* בְּרָא) field (186).

בְּרַך   to kneel *D 6:11.*

בְּרַך   *pa.* to bless (20, *115*).

בְּרַך*   knee.

בְּרַם   but (*85*).

בְּשַׂר   flesh, mankind (*52*, 95, 96).

בַּת*   (pl. בַּתִּין) bath (*liquid measure*).

בְּתַר   *see* בָּאתַר.

ג

גַּב*   *see* גּוּב*.

גֹּב   (*det.* גֻּבָּא) den, pit (10, 20, 48, 78).

גְּבוּרָה*   power (31).

גְּבַר   (pl. גֻּבְרִין) man (30, 38, 48, *51*, 95, 184).

גִּבָּר*   strong man (27).

גְּדָבַר*   treasurer (17, *189*).

גדד   to cut down (10, *160*).

גּוֹא   (מִן גּ׳, בְּגִ׳, לְגִ׳) midst, inside (*prep.*) (5, *84*).

גֵּוָה   arrogance (10).

גּוּח   *hap.* to stir up (*141*).

גִּזְבַּר   (*pl. det.* גִּזְבְּרַיָּא) treasurer (17, *189*).

גזר   *hitp.* to break off (*intrans.*) (104, *117*).

גָּזַר*   exorcizer (*or some other kind of practitioner of super-natural craft*).

גְּזֵרָה*   decision.

גִּיר*   plaster, whitewash.

גַּלְגַּל*   (*pl. suff.* גַּלְגִּלּוֹהִי) wheel (*of a chair*).

גלה   to reveal; *hap.* to exile (10, *146*, 184).

גָּלוּ*   exile (*55*, 80).

גְּלָל   (אֶבֶן גְּלָל) hewn stone.

גְּמִיר   completely (*88*).

גַּב*   (*suff.* גַּבֵּיהּ) side.

גְּנַז*   (*pl. det.* גִּנְזַיָּא) treasure (*189*).

גַּף*   (pl. גַּפִּין) wing (59).

גְּרַם*   bone.

גְּשֵׁם*   body (*51*).

ד

דְ   *see* דִי.
דָא   this (*fem.*) (17, 30, *32*, *33*).
דֹב   bear.
דבח   to sacrifice (17).
דְּבַח*   sacrifice.
דבק   to adhere.
דִּבְרַת   (עַל [עַד] דִּי דִּי) so that (*86*).
דְּהַב   gold (16, 17, 30, 46, *52*).
דְּהַוָא   *read* דְהוּא (*35*).
דוֹר   to dwell (12, 59, 87, *137*).
דּוּרָא   Dura (*name of a locality*).
דוֹשׁ   to trample upon.
דַּחֲוָן   table? (*other traditional guesses consider the word a pl. fem.:* concubines, food, musical instruments, perfume *D 6:19*).
דחל   to fear, (דְּחִיל) frightful; *pa.* to frighten (40, 88).
דִּי   *relative pronoun, subordinating conjunction* (16, 17, 30, 35—37, 46, *48*, 62, 80, 83—85, *86*, 91, 95, 177, 184, 186).
-דִּי לְ   *independent possessive pronoun* (*31*).
דִּי לָא   without (*prep.*) (*84*, 87).
דִּי לְמָה   lest (*86*).
דִּין   to judge (*137*).
דִּין   justice, court, law suit, judgment.
דַּיָּן*   judge (40).
דִּינָיֵא   *read* דַּיָּנַיָּא judges *E 4:9*.
דֵּךְ   (*fem.* דָךְ) that (*demonstrative pronoun*) (*32*, 87, 177).
דִּכֵּן   that (*demonstrative pronoun*) (*32*).
דְּכַר*   ram.
דִּכְרוֹן*   memorandum (22).
דִּכְרָן   memorandum, (סְפַר דָּכְרָנַיָּא) record book (10, 17, 22, 27).
דלק   to burn.
דמה   to resemble.
דְּנָה   this (16, 17, *32*—*34*, 47, 78, 82, 92, 96, 177, 184).
דָּנִיֵּאל   Daniel (*13*, 30, 76, 77, 82, 89).
דקק   to be crushed; *haṗ.* to crush (10, 104, 117, *158*, *164*).

דָּר   generation (83).

דָּרְיָוֹשׁ   Darius (< *OPers. Dārayavauš*) (26, 178).

דְּרָע*   arm.

דָּת   law, legal situation (30, *59*, 78, *189*).

דִּתְאָ*   vegetation, grass (186).

דְּתָבַר*   law official (16, *189*).

ה

הַ, הֲ   *introducing questions* (30, 93, *94*, 95).

הָא   behold (*91*).

הֵא כְדִי   as (*conj.*) (*86*).

הַדָּבַר*   companion (*189*).

הַדָּם*   limb (*189*).

הדר   *pa.* to glorify.

הֲדַר*   glory.

הוּא   he, that (*demonstrative pronoun*) (13, *29*, *30*, *32*, 33, *34*, 35).

הוה   to be (10, 79, *132*, *145*, *147*, *148*, *168*, *177*).

הוּךְ   to go (*134*, *136*, *169*, 178).

הִיא   she (13, *29*, *30*, 31).

הֵיכַל   palace, temple (*188*).

הֵימָן   *see* אמן.

הֵיתִי   *see* אתה.

הלךְ   *pa.*, *hap̄.* to walk about (*169*).

הֲלָךְ   a kind of taxes (85, *188*).

הִמּוֹ   they, them (26, *29*, *30*, 84, 174, 184).

הִמּוֹן   them (*29*, 174, 184).

הַמוֹנֻךְ*   (*det. q°rē̆* הַמְנִיכָא, correctly *הַמְיָנַךְ) necklace (*189*).

הֵן   if, (הֵן ··· הֵן) either . . . or (*86*, 95).

הַצְדָּא   really? (*93*).

הַרְהֹר*   (*pl.*) imaginings (39).

ו

וְ   and (27, 30, 46, 47, 63, 74, 76, 78, 81, 83, 84, *85*, 86, 89, 177—179, 181, 184).

ז

זְבַן	to buy.
זְהִיר*	warned, careful (*not to do something*).
זוד	*see* זיד.
זוּן	*hitp.* to obtain food, to feed (*138*).
זוּע	to tremble (17).
זיד (זוד)	*hap.* to act impiously (*142*).
זִיו*	facial features, radiant healthy complexion, splendor (10, *188*).
זָכוּ	innocence (*18, 188*).
זְכַרְיָה	Zechariah.
זְמַן	*hitp.* to agree upon (*114*).
זְמַן	time, (בֵּה זִמְנָא) at the very time, moment (*52, 89*).
זְמָר*	music (46).
זַמָּר*	musician (40).
זַן*	kind, species (46, *189*).
זְעֵיר*	small.
זְעִק	(e/i) to shout, to call.
זְקִיף	crucified.
זְרֻבָּבֶל	Zerubbabel.
זְרַע	seed, semen.

ח

חֲבוּלָה	harm, damage.
חֲבַל	*pa.* to harm, to damage, to destroy; *hitpa.* to be destroyed.
חֲבָל	damage, harm.
חֲבַר*	colleague (*52*).
חַבְרָה*	(*fem.*) colleague, counterpart (80).
חַגַּי	Haggai.
חַד	one (30, *46, 63, 64, 70*, 78, 80, 82). *See also* כַּחֲדָה.
חֲדֶה*	breast (*54*).
חֶדְוָה	joy (*55*).
חֲדַת	new.
חֲוָה	*pa., hap.* to tell, to inform someone about something (10, *111, 132, 147, 153, 176*).
חוּט, חִיט	*see* יחט.

חִוָּר	white.
חֲזָה	to see, (חֲזֵה) seeming, appropriate, usual (91, *116*).
חֵזוּ*	vision, appearance (*55*, 80, 83).
חֲזוֹת*	appearance (*55*).
חטא	*pa.* to make a sin-offering (*187*).
חֲטָא*	sin (*14*).
חַי	(*det.* חַיָּא) living, alive, living being (30, 80).
חיה	to live; *haṗ.* to let live, to keep alive (43, 79, *148*, *170*).
חֵיוָה	animal, animals (15, 34, *49*, 83, 184).
חַיִּין	life (79).
חַיִל	strength, might, force, army, (בְּחַיִל) aloud (25, 27, *51*).
חַכִּים	wise, sage (40).
חָכְמָה	wisdom (16, 31, *51*, 80, 84, 95).
חֵלֶם	dream (34, *51*).
חֲלַף	to pass by.
חֲלָק	share, tax revenue.
חֲמָה, חֱמָה	wrath.
חֲמַר	wine (46, *51*).
חִנְטָה*	(*pl.* חִנְטִין) wheat (*61*).
חֲנֻכָּה*	inauguration.
חנן	to show mercy; *hitpa.* to seek mercy (*161*).
חֲנַנְיָה	Hananiah.
חַסִּיר	wanting, deficient.
חסן	*haṗ.* to possess, to take possession of (*116*).
חֲסַן*	(det. חִסְנָא) power.
חֲסַף	clay, earthenware.
חצף	*haṗ. part. pass.* urgent (*116*).
חרב	*haṗ.* to destroy (10, *116*).
חַרְטֹם	(*pl. det.* חַרְטֻמַיָּא) magician (*23*, *187*).
חֲרַךְ	*hitpa.* to be scorched.
חֲרַץ*	(*suff.* חַרְצֵהּ) hip, loins.
חֲשַׁב	to consider (87).
חֲשׁוֹךְ*	darkness.
חֲשַׁח*	needed, needing (*44*, 188).
חַשְׁחוּ*	needs (*56*).
חֲשַׁל	to smash.
חתם	to seal.

ט

טאב	(e/i) to be good, (טְאֵב עֲלֹוהִי) it pleased him (82, *125*, 128).
טָב	good (17, 22, *42*, 128).
טַבָּח*	butcher, executioner (17, 40).
טוּר	mountain (17, 79).
טְוָת	fasting (*adv.*) (*88*).
טִין*	clay.
טַל	dew (17, 76).
טלל	*hap.* to seek shade (shelter) (17, *157*).
טעם	*pa.* to feed (*trans.*) (181).
טְעֵם, טַעַם	order, decree, information, attention, influence (*of wine*) (*51*, 80, 178, *188*). *See also* בְּעֵל.
טְפַר*	fingernail, claw (17).
טרד	to drive out (181).
טַרְפְּלָיֵא	*meaning?* (*191*).

י

יבל	*hap.* (הֵיבֵל) to bring (*130*). *See also* סובל.
יַבֶּשָׁה*	(*det.* יַבֶּשְׁתָּא) dry land.
יְגַר	heap of stones.
יַד	hand (10, 17, 25, 26, 36, *45*, *59*, *84*).
ידה	*hap.* to laud (*130*).
ידע	to know; *hap.* to let know (10, 17, 21, 26, 88, 111, 117, *128—130*, 174, 175, 177).
יהב	to give, to lay (*foundations*); *hitp.* to be given (36, 80, 84, 118, *129*, 179).
יְהוּד	Judaea (76).
יְהוּדִי*	Jew, Jewish (42, *58*, 83, 95).
יֹום	(*pl.* יֹומָן*, יֹומִין) day (*62*, *74*, 80, 81, 177).
יֹוצָדָק	Jozadak.
יחט (?)	*pa.* to lay (*foundations?*) (*178*).
יטב	to be good, it pleases (*128*).
יכל	(e/i) to be able, to prevail (*128*, *171*).
יַם*	(*det.* יַמָּא) sea.
יסף	*hap.* to add (27, *130*).
יעט	*hitpa.* to take counsel with each other, to agree after mutual consultation.

יָעֵט*   adviser (17, 66).

יצב   pa. to make certain.

יַצִּיב   certain, (יַצִּיבָא) certainly (88).

יָקֵד*   fiery, burning.

יְקֵדָה*   burning, conflagration (10).

יַקִּיר*   important, difficult.

יְקָר   (יְקָר‏ ?‏ D 4:33) honor.

יְרוּשְׁלֵם   Jerusalem (76, 84).

יְרַח   month (74).

יְרֵךּ*   (יִרְכָה* ?‏, pl. suff. יַרְכָתֵהּ) thigh (51).

יִשְׂרָאֵל   Israel (47, 75, 80, 187).

יֵשׁוּעַ   Jeshua.

יָת*   prep. introducing the direct object (31, 84).

יתב   (e/i) to sit, to be settled; hap̄. to settle (trans.) (10, 17, 128, 130).

יַתִּיר   excessive, (יַתִּירָא, יַתִּירָא) excessively (88).

כ

כְּ   like as, comparable to, according to (16, 33, 74, 75, 78, 84, 87, 92, 149, 181). See also כְּעַן, כַּחֲדָה, כְּדִי, כְּעֵת, כְּעֶנֶת.

כְּדַב*   (fem. כִּדְבָה) untrue (15).

כְּדִי   when (78, 86). See also הֵא כְּדִי.

כָּה   here (81, 91).

כהל   (e/i?) to be able (95, 171).

כָּהֵן*   priest (187).

כַּוָּה*   (pl. כַּוִּין) window (61).

כֹּורֶשׁ   Cyrus (< OPers. Kūruš) (26).

כַּחֲדָה   together, without distinction (64, 93).

כַּכַּר*   talent (monetary unit) (81).

כֹּל   (כֹּלָא, כָּל) totality, every, entire, all (10, 26, 36, 46, 47, 49, 80, 84, 85, 87, 88, 96).

כָּל קֳבֵל   see קֳבֵל.

כְּלַל   see שִׁכְלַל.

כְּמָה   how! (92).

כֵּן   thus (92).

כְּנָת*   (כְּנָת* ?) colleague (62, 188).

כְּנֵמָא thus (26, *92*).

כנש to assemble (*trans.*); *hitpa.* to assemble (*intrans.*) (177).

כַּסְדְּי* *see* כַּשְׂדְּי.

כְּסַף silver (46, *51*, 81).

כְּעַן (כְּעֶת, כְּעֶנֶת) now, now then (*89*, 183).

כפת to bind; *pa.* to bind (10).

כֹּר* kor (*solid measure*).

כַּרְבְּלָה* hat (*189*).

כרה *hitp.* to become sick, sad (*151*).

כָּרוֹז* herald (40, 177).

כרז* *hap̄.* to announce publicly.

כָּרְסֵא (*pl.* כָּרְסָוָן) chair, throne (10, *54*, *188*).

כַּשְׂדְּי (כַּס׳) Chaldaean (14, 19, *58*).

כתב to write (17, 23, 26, *101*, *105*, *110*, *111*, 177).

כְּתָב writing, text, document, letter, stipulation in writing

כְּתַל (*pl. det.* כְּתָלַיָּא) wall (*of a house*) (51). [(78).

ל

לְ to, for (5, 10, 27, 31, 33, 36, 43, *47*, 49, 74, *75*, 76, 78, *79*, 84—86, 111, 118, 171, 177—179, 181, *182*, 187).

לָא not, (לָה) nought (30, 59, 77, 85, 86, *87*, 94, 95). *See also* דִּי לָא.

לֵב* (*suff.* לִבִּי) heart.

לְבַב* heart (83).

לְבוּשׁ* garment (10).

לבש to be dressed, to wear; *hap̄.* to dress (*trans.*) (10).

לָה *see* לָא.

לְהֵוֵא (לֶהֱוָן, לֶהֱוֹן) *see* הוה (*168*).

לָהֵן but, except (*85*).

לֵוִי* Levite (*187*).

לְוָת* with, at (*chez*) (84).

לְחֵם meal, banquet (*51*).

לְחֵנָה* maid servant (10).

לֵילְיָא* (*det.* לֵילְיָא) night (*54*, 83, 89).

לָמָה lest (*86*, 87). *See also* דִּי לָמָה.

לְקָבֵל *see* קְבֵל.

לְשָׁן* tongue, language.

מ

מְ-	see מִן.
מְאָה	hundred (*63*, 81).
מֹאזַנְיָה	(מֹאזַנְיָה) (*pl. det.*) scales (13).
מָאן*	vessel (13, 34, 46, 184).
מָאתַיִן	two hundred (13, *45*, *63*).
מְגִלָּה	scroll (46).
מגר	*pa.* to overthrow.
מַדְבַּח*	altar (17).
מִדָּה	see מִנְדָּה.
מָדוֹר*	(מְדוֹר*?) dwelling (22).
מָדַי	Media (< *OPers. Māda, through Akk. Madai*) (78).
מָדָי*	Median.
מְדִינָה*	province (10, 15, 48).
מְדָר	dwelling (22, 95).
מָה	what?, whatever (*37*, *38*). *See also* כְּמָה.
מוֹת	death (86).
מָזוֹן	food (17, 23).
מחא	to hit; *pa.* to hit, (יְמַחֵא בִידֵהּ) to stay (His hand); *hitpa.* to be beaten, to be affixed (17).
מַחְלְקָה*	division, group.
מטא, מטה	to come, to go (*76*, 81).
מִישָׁאֵל	Mishael.
מֵישַׁךְ	Meshach.
מלא	to fill; *hitp.* to be filled.
מַלְאַךְ*	angel (*187*).
מִלָּה	(*pl.* מִלִּין) word, speech, matter (33, 47, *61*, 84, 86, 90).
מלח	to partake of salt.
מְלַח	salt (*51*).
מֶלֶךְ	king (15, 32, 36, 40, 42, 43, 47, *51*, 62, 79, 80, 82—84, 88, 90, 99, 111, 177, *189*).
מִלַךְ*	(*suff.* מִלְכִּי) advice (*51*).
מַלְכָּה*	queen (*51*).
מַלְכוּ	kingdom, reign (36, 40, 47, *56*, 74, 79, 84, 89, 179).
מלל	*pa.* to speak (10, 24, 83, 84).
מַן	who?, (מַן דִּי) whoever (30, *37*, *38*).

מִן (מֵ-)	from (17, 20, 33, 64, *75*, 76, *80*, 81, 84—86, 88, 89, 91, 177, 181).
מִן דִּי	as soon as, after (*conj.*) (*86*).
מְנֵא	mina (*monetary unit*) (*188*).
מִנְדָּה, מִדָּה	a kind of taxes (*188*).
מַנְדַּע	knowledge (21, 82, 128).
מנה	to count, to number; *pa.* to appoint (26, *153*).
מִנְחָה	(sacrificial) offering (*187*).
מִנְיָן	number.
מַעֲבָד*	work, deed (10, 36).
מְעֵה*	belly (*54*).
מֶעָל*	entrance, (מֶעָלֵי שִׁמְשָׁא) sunset (159).
מָרֵא	lord, master (13, *54*, *62*).
מְרַד	rebellion (177).
מָרָד*	rebellious (15).
מרט	to pluck out, to tear off.
מֹשֶׁה	Moses (78).
מְשַׁח	oil.
מִשְׁכַּב*	bed.
מִשְׁכַּן*	dwelling.
מַשְׁרוֹקִי*	pipe (*musical instr.*) (46, *57*).
מִשְׁתֵּא*	banquet (40).
מַתְּנָה*	gift (17).

נ

נבא	*hitpa.* to prophesy.
נְבוּאָה*	prophecy, prophetical office (187).
נְבוּכַדְנֶצַּר	Nebuchadnezzar (*Akk. Nabu-kudurri-uṣur*) (84).
נְבִזְבָּה	(*pl. suff.* נְבִזְבְּיָתָךְ) gift (*62*, *190*).
נְבִיא*	prophet (*187*).
נִבְרְשָׁה*	(*det.* נִבְרַשְׁתָּא) lamp (*190*).
נגד	to flow.
נֶגֶד	toward (*84*).
נֹגַהּ*	(*det.* נָגְהָא) dawn (*51*, 186).
נְגוֹ	*see* עֲבַד נְגוֹ.
נדב	*hitpa.* to volunteer, to contribute voluntarily (111).
נִדְבָּךְ	layer (*of a building*) (*188*).

נדד   to flee (*158*).

גְדָן*   (נִדְנֶה, *read* נִדְנֶה) container, sheath (10, *190*).

נְהוֹר*   (*det. k^ᵉtīḇ* נהירא, *q^ᵉrē* נְהוֹרָא) light.

נְהִירוּ   brilliance (*56*).

נְהַר   river (188).

נוד   to flee.

נְוָלוּ, נְוָלִי   dunghill (*57*, *190*).

נוּר   fire (*59*, 184).

נזק   to suffer harm, to suffer damage; *haṗ.* to harm, to cause damage to (99, *111*).

נְחָשׁ   copper.

נחת   to go down, to descend; *haṗ.* to bring down, to deposit (184).

נטל   to lift up (178).

נטר   to guard (17).

נִיחוֹחִין   sacrifices of sweet smell (*187*).

נְכַס*   (*pl.* נִכְסִין) possessions, property (47, 86, *188*).

נְמַר   panther.

נסח   *hitpa.* to be torn out.

נסך   *pa.* to pour out (*libations*).

נְסַך   (*pl. suff.* נִסְכֵּיהוֹן) libation (*51*, *187*).

נפל   to fall, to be necessary (10, 12, *118*).

נפק   to go out, to come out; *haṗ.* to take out, to bring out (*119*, 177).

נִפְקָה*   expenses (80).

נִצְבָּה*   seed, planting, mineral (*traditional:* strength) (80).

נצח   *hitpa.* to distinguish oneself (82).

נצל   *haṗ.* to save.

נְקֵא   clean, pure.

נקשׁ   to knock.

נשׂא   to lift up, to take, to carry; *hitpa.* to rise up (82, *118*, *119*, *126*, 177, 184).

נְשִׁין*   (*suff.* נְשֵׁיהוֹן) *see* אַנְתָּה.

נִשְׁמָה*   breath, soul (36, 84).

נְשַׁר   eagle.

נִשְׁתְּוָן*   written order (*189*).

נְתִין*   temple servant (*187*).

נתן   to give (*118*, 129, 175).

נתר   *haṗ.* to shake off (*115*).

ס

סַבֵּךְ*	see *שַׂבֵּךְ.
סבר	to hope, to intend (19).
סגד	(e/i) to prostrate oneself (*102, 106*).
סְגַן*	(*pl.* סְגְנִין) prefect (*188*).
סגר	to lock (10, 85).
סובל	*part. pass.* (מְסוֹבְלִין) laid (*foundations*) (*130*, 166, *188*).
סוּמְפֹּנְיָה	(סיפניה) symphony (bagpipe?) (*46, 191*).
סוֹף	to end, to cease; *haṗ.* to make an end to (26, *141*).
סוֹף	end.
סיפניה	see סוּמְפֹּנְיָה.
סלק	(e/i) to go up, to come up; *haṗ.* to bring up (21, 23,
סעד	*pa.* to help (20). [*172*).
סְפַר	book, document (27, *51*, 78).
סְפַר*	scribe, secretary.
סַרְבָּל*	trousers (*189*).
סָרֵךְ*	chief minister (82, *189*).
סתר	*pa.* to conceal (*44*).
סתר	to tear down (19, 184).

ע

עבד	to do, to make; *hitṗ.* to be made, to be done (10, 27, 83, *116*, 177, 189).
עֲבֵד	servant, slave (29, 30, *51*).
עֲבֵד נְגוֹ	Abed-nego.
עֲבִידָה*	work, administration, service, worship (15, 17, 48).
עֲבַר נַהֲרָא	across-the-River, Trans-Euphrates Province (Syria) (*188*).
עַד	until (*prep.*) (75, 76, *81*, 89). *See also* דִּבְרַת.
עַד, עַד דִּי	until (*conj.*) (*86, 178*).
עדה	to come forth, to pass away, to become invalid; *haṗ.* to remove (59, *76, 116*, 184).
עִדּוֹא	Iddo (*5*).
עִדָּן	time, season (year) (*66*, 86).
עוֹד	still, yet (*90*).
עֲוָיָה	iniquity, misdeed.
עוֹף	bird, birds.

עוּר　　chaff.

*עֵז　　(pl. עִזִּין) goat (59).

*עִזְקָה　　seal ring.

עֶזְרָא　　Ezra.

עֲזַרְיָה　　Azariah.

עֵטָה　　advice, counsel (10, 17, 129).

*עַיִן　　eye (51, 59, 178).

עִיר　　a kind of angel.

עַל　　upon (10, 26, 33, 49, 75, 76, 82, 84, 86, 177, 178).

עֵלָּא　　above (adv.) (80, 88).

עִלָּה　　cause, pretext.

*עֲלָוָה　　sacrifice (79).

*עִלָּי　　most high (84).

*עִלִּי　　(suff. עִלִּיתֵהּ) upper room (57).

*עֶלְיוֹן　　most high (22, 179, 187).

עלל　　to enter; hap̄. to let enter (17, 20, 26, 76, 158, 162, 164,

עָלַם　　eternity (43, 53, 62, 79, 80, 177).　　　　　　[175).

*עֵלְמָי　　Elamite.

*עֲלַע　　(pl. עִלְעִין) rib (17, 59).

עַם　　(det. עַמָּא, pl. עַמְמַיָּא) people (17, 20, 62, 179, 184).

עִם　　(together) with (75, 76, 83, 95).

*עַמִּיק　　deep (44).

עֲמַר　　wool (17).

עָן　　(עֵת, עֵנֶת*) see כְּעַן, etc.

ענה　　to answer (150).

*עֲנֵה　　humble, poor (25).

*עֲנָן　　cloud.

*עֲנַף　　branch (of a tree).

עֲנַשׁ　　fine (punishment) (47, 86).

*עֳפִי　　(suff. עָפְיֵהּ) foliage (51).

עֲצִיב　　sad.

עקר　　hiṯp. to be uprooted (115).

עִקַּר　　(עִקָּר) offshoot.

*עַר　　(עֲרָר ?, pl. suff. עָרָיִךְ) adversary (17).

ערב　　pa. to mix (trans.); hiṯpa. to mix (intrans.) (76).

*עֲרָד　　onager, wild ass.

*עֶרְוָה　　nakedness, shame.

עֲשַׂב　　vegetation, grass (75, 181, 186).

עֲשַׂר ten (45, *63*).

עֶשְׂרִין twenty (*63*).

עֲשִׁית concerned about.

עָתִיד* ready, prepared (95).

עַתִּיק old (81).

פ

פֶּחָה (*pl.* *פַּחֲוָן) governor (36, *62, 188*).

פֶּחָר potter.

פְּטִישׁ* shirt (?) (*189*).

פלג to divide.

פְּלַג half (*71*).

פְּלֻגָּה* section, group.

פלח to serve, to worship (36, 85, 95, *115*).

פָּלְחָן service, worship, cult (10).

פֻּם (*suff.* פֻּמֵּהּ) mouth (20, 90).

פַּס palm (of a hand, *or some other* part of a hand).

פְּסַנְתֵּרִין (פְּסַנְטֵ') psaltery (16, *46, 191*).

פַּרְזֶל iron (39, *188*).

פרס to divide.

פְּרֵס half-mina (*or* half-shekel) (*monetary unit*) (*188*).

פָּרַס Persia (< *O Pers.* Pārsa).

פָּרְסִי* Persian.

פרק to atone for, redeem.

פרשׁ *pa.* to interpret.

פַּרְשֶׁגֶן copy (*51, 189*).

פְּשַׁר to interpret; *pa.* (?) to interpret (*111*).

פְּשַׁר interpretation (*51*).

פִּתְגָּם message, word, matter (15, *189*).

פתח to open (61).

פְּתִי* breadth (*54*).

צ

צבה (*e/i*) to want, to wish (17, *145, 149*).

צְבוּ thing, matter (*55, 77*).

צבע *pa.* to wet; *hitpa.* to be wetted (*76, 114*).

צַד   side (*84*).

*צְדָא   *see* הַצְדָּא.

צְדָקָה   charity.

*צַוַּאר   neck (*13*).

צלה   *pa.* to pray (79).

צלח   *hap.* to make successful, to prosper (*intrans.*), to succeed (17, *111*).

צֶלֶם, צְלֵם   image, statue, complexion (17, 32, 34, 46, *51*).

*צְפִיר   (צְפִירֵי עִזִּין) he-goat.

*צִפַּר   bird (10, *59*).

ק

קבל   *pa.* to receive, to take over.

קֳבֵל   (כָּל קֳבֵל, לָקֳבֵל) facing, opposite, corresponding to
(*prep.*), (כָּל קֳבֵל דִּי) because (*conj.*) (10, 33, *84*, *86*,
96, 177).

*קַדִּישׁ   holy, saint (83, 179).

קֳדָם   before (*prep.*) (*10*, 25, 80, *84*, 85).

*קַדְמָי   first (*69*).

קַדְמַת   (מִן קָ׳, מְקָ׳) before (*prep.*) (*84*, 177).

קום   to stand, to arise, to last; *pa.* to establish; *hap.* to set
up, to install, to appoint, to issue (*an interdict*) (14,
23, 117, *133—137*, *139—142*, 177).

קטל   to kill; *pa.* to kill; *hitp., hitpa.* to be killed (184).

*קְטַר   (*pl.* קִטְרִין) knot, joint, difficult problem.

קַיִט   summer (17, 26, *51*).

קְיָם   statute.

קַיָּם   enduring.

קִיתָרוֹס   (*q°rē* קַתְ׳) zither (*46*, *191*).

קָל   sound, voice (46).

קנה   to purchase.

קצף   to become angry (88).

קְצַף   wrath.

קצץ   *pa.* to cut off.

קְצָת   end, part (80, *84*).

קרא   to call, to call out, to read aloud, to read; *hitp.* to be
called (10, *108*, *146*, *152*, 177).

קְרֵב (e/i) to draw near, to approach; pa. to offer (sacrifices); hap̄. to bring near, to offer (sacrifices) (10, 26, 78).

קְרָב war (83, 188).

קִרְיָה* (pl. det. קִרְיָה) city (62, 87, 177).

קֶרֶן horn (of animals, musical instrument) (45, 46, 51, 59).

קְרָץ* piece, (*אֲכַל קַרְצִין) to denounce, to slander (cf. Akk.).

קְשֹׁט truth (10, 36, 51, 80, 86).

ר

רֵאשׁ head, chief (13, 17, 30, 62).

רַב (det. רַבָּא, pl. רַבְרְבִין) great, big, (pl. *רַבְרְבָנִין) chief, magnate (44, 47, 59, 61, 62, 80, 92).

רבה to grow; pa. to make someone a magnate (145).

רְבוּ greatness (55).

רִבּוֹ (pl. kᵉṯib̄ רבבן) myriad (62, 63).

רְבִיעָי* fourth (69).

רגז hap̄. to anger.

רְגַז anger (51).

רְגַל* foot (45, 59).

רגשׁ hap̄. to assemble (intrans.).

רוּ* appearance.

רוּחַ wind, spirit (59).

רום (e/i) to be high, to be haughty; hap̄. to raise up; *רוֹמֵם to exalt; *הִתְרוֹמֵם to exalt oneself (23, 133, 141, 143, 157).

רוּם* height.

רָז secret, mystery (16, 82, 189).

רְחוּם Rehum.

רַחִיק* remote.

רַחֲמִין mercy.

רחץ hitp̄. to trust.

רֵיחַ smell (59).

רמה to throw, to set up (chairs), to impose (taxes); hitp̄. to be thrown.

רְעוּ* wish, pleasure (17, 55).

רַעְיוֹן* thought (22).

רַעֲנַן   relaxed.

רעע   to break; *pa.* to break, to crush (20, *159*).

רפס   to trample upon.

רשַׁם   to draw, to draw up, to inscribe, to write.

שׂ

שָׂב*   elder (83).

שַׂבְּכָא*   ('ס) sambuke (harp) (19, 46).

שׂגא   to be (become) much (great).

שַׂגִּיא   much, many, great, (*adv.*) much, greatly, very (13, 61, *88*, 177).

שָׂהֲדוּ*   testimony (*56*).

שְׂטַר   side (46).

שׂים   to place, to set, to appoint, to give (*an order, a name*), to pay (*attention*); *hitp.* to be placed, to be made, to be given (*order*) (36, 80, 82, 117, *133—136, 138*).

שׂכל   *hitpa.* to observe (*114*).

שָׂכְלְתָנוּ   intelligence (*56*).

שָׂנֵא*   enemy (13, *126*).

שְׂעַר   hair.

שׁ

שׁאל   (*e/i*) to ask (17, 24, 26, *125*, 175).

שְׁאֵלָה*   question, problem (15).

שְׁאַלְתִּיאֵל   Shealtiel.

שְׁאָר   rest, remnant (184).

שׁבח   *pa.* to praise (24, *115*, *117*).

שֵׁבֶט*   tribe (*187*).

שְׁבִיב*   flame (184).

שְׁבַע*   seven (*63, 66, 70*, 82).

שׁבק   to leave; *hitp.* to be left (26, *114*).

שׁבשׁ   *hitpa.* to be confused (*114*).

שֵׁגְלָה*   concubine (*188*).

שׁדר   *hitpa.* to make efforts (111).

שַׁדְרַךְ   Shadrach.

שׁוה   *pa.* to make equal, to place; *hitpa.* to be made (83, *132*).

שׁוּר*   wall (*of a city*) (178).

שׁוּשַׁנְכָּי*   man from Susa (< *OPers.* *Šūšānaka).

שְׁחִית   corrupt, (*fem.*) fault, corruption (*44*).

שֵׁיזֵב   to save (10, 49, 84, *166*, 175, *188*).

שֵׁיצִי(א)   to complete (*18*, *166*, *188*).

שְׁכַח   *hitp.* to be found; *hap.* to find (26, *114*, *115*, *117*).

שְׁכְלֵל   to complete; *hištapʿal* to be completed (*157*, 166, 178, *188*).

שְׁכֵן   to dwell; *pa.* to cause to dwell.

שְׁלֵה   happy, carefree.

שְׁלוּ, שָׁלָה   negligence (*55*).

שְׁלֵוָה*   happiness.

שְׁלַח   to send, to send a message (*by messenger, letter*) (82).

שְׁלֵט   (*e/i*) to rule, to have power over, to overpower; *hap.* to give power to (*76*, *102*, *110*).

שָׁלְטָן*   authority, official (22).

שָׁלְטָן   rule, domination, dominion (22, 184).

שַׁלִּיט   (*adj.*) mighty, powerful, being in control, authorized, (*noun*) (*powerful*) official (10, 17, 40).

שְׁלִם   (*e/i*) to be completed; *hap.* to finish, to bring to an end, to hand over (*102*).

שְׁלָם   well-being, greetings (96).

שֵׁם   (*pl.* *שְׁמָהָן) name (30, 36, 38, 48, *62*).

שְׁמַד   *hap.* to exterminate.

שְׁמַיִן*   (*det.* שְׁמַיָּא) heaven (17, 36, 47, 59, 75, 84, 178).

שְׁמַם   (אֶשְׁתּוֹמַם) to be perturbed (*157*).

שְׁמַע   to hear; *hitpa.* to obey (17).

שָׁמְרַיִן*   (*pausal* שָׁמְרָיִן) Samaria (25, 62).

שַׁמֵּשׁ   *pa.* to serve.

שְׁמֵשׁ*   (*det.* שִׁמְשָׁא) sun (*51*).

שִׁמְשַׁי   Shimshai.

שֵׁן*   (dual שִׁנַּיִן) tooth (*45*, 59).

שְׁנָה   to be different, to change (*intrans.*); *pa.* to cause a change, to change (*trans.*), to distinguish; *hitpa.* to change (*intrans.*); *hap.* to change (*trans.*) (77, *108*, *150*, *152*).

שְׁנָה*   (*pl.* שְׁנִין) year (30, *61*, *74*, 78, 177).

שְׁנָה*   (*suff.* שְׁנָתֵהּ) sleep (129).

שָׁעָה   hour, while, (בַּהּ שַׁעֲתָא) at this very hour, moment (46, 62, 78, *89*, 177).

שְׁפֵט*   judge (*18*, 187).

שַׁפִּיר   beautiful.

שפל   *hap̄.* to bring down, to humiliate, to humble (10).

שְׁפַל   low.

שפר   to be good, it pleases.

שְׁפַרְפָּר*   dawn (39, 186).

שָׁק*   leg.

שרה   to loosen, to unfetter, to explain (*knotty problems*), to reside (שָׁרֵה residing); *pa.* to solve (?), to begin; *hitpa.* to be loosened (*111, 150*).

שְׁרֹשׁ*   (*pl. suff.* שָׁרְשׁוֹהִי) root (*51*).

שׁרשׁו   (*q°rē* שָׁרֹשִׁי) corporal punishment (19, *57*, 86, *189*).

שֵׁשְׁבַּצַּר   Sheshbazzar (= שנאבצר* ?, *Akk. Sin-ab-uṣur*).

שֵׁת, שֵׁת   six (*63*, 74).

שתה   (*e/i,* אֶשְׁתִּי*) to drink (46, *77*, *145*, *150*, *173*).

שִׁתִּין   sixty (*63*, 74, 78).

שְׁתַר בּוֹזְנַי   Shethar-bozenai (= שתברזן, < *O Pers. Šatibrjana* "desiring joy").

ת

תְּבִיר*   fragile.

תְּדִיר*   (בִּתְדִירָא) constantly.

תוב   to return (*intrans.*); *hap̄.* to return (*trans.*) (82, *141*, *142*, 178, 184).

תוה   to be perturbed (*132*).

תּוֹר*   ox (17, 181).

תְּחוֹת, תַּחַת*   underneath (*prep.*) (22, 47, *84*).

תְּלַג   snow (*51*).

תְּלִיתָי*   third (14, *69*).

תְּלָת*   (*det.* תְּלָתָא) triumvir (*71*, *188*).

תְּלָת   three, (תְּלָתֵהוֹן) the three of them (17, 22, 23, 59, *63*, 66, *73*, 74).

תְּלָתִין   thirty (*63*, 81).

תַּמָּה   there (17, *91*).

תְּמַהּ*   wonder (92).

תִּנְיָן*   second (69).

תִּנְיָנוּת   again (72, 88).

תִּפְתָּ*   (pl. det. תִּפְתָּיֵא) police chief (58, 189).

תַּקִּיף*   strong, powerful (88, 92).

תקל   to weigh.

תְּקֵל   shekel (monetary unit).

תקן   hap̄. to restore.

תקף   (e/i) to be (become) strong; pa. to strengthen, to issue a strong (prohibition) (102).

תְּקָף   (det. תָּקְפָּא) strength (10, 51).

תְּרֵין*   (fem. תַּרְתֵּין) two (45, 63, 65, 74, 78).

תְּרַע   door, gate, (royal) court (17).

תָּרָע*   doorkeeper (20, 40).

תַּרְתֵּין   see * תְּרֵין.

תַּתְּנַי   Tattenai (Akk. Tattannai).